THE UNOFFICIAL NARNIA COOKBOOK

FROM TURKISH DELIGHT

TO GOOSEBERRY FOOL—OVER 150 RECIPES INSPIRED

BY THE CHRONICLES OF NARNIA

DINAH BUCHOLZ

sourcebooks
jabberwocky

To the memory of my beloved grandmother, Mima.
She spoke seven languages, had a most elegant handwriting,
and was an awesome cook.

Published by Sourcebooks Jabberwocky, an imprint of Sourcebooks, Inc.
P.O. Box 4410, Naperville, Illinois 60567-4410
(630) 961-3900
Fax: (630) 961-2168
www.jabberwockykids.com

Library of Congress Cataloging-in-Publication data is on file with the publisher.

Source of Production: Bang Printing, Brainerd, Minnesota, USA
Date of Production: October 2012
Run Number: 18522

Printed and bound in the United States of America.
BG 10 9 8 7 6 5 4 3 2 1

CONTENTS

ACKNOWLEDGMENTS

First, I thank God, who is the source of all blessings. Second, I thank my idol. That's my husband, Heshy. Joking aside, it's thanks to him that this book ever got written. He had borrowed *The Magician's Nephew* on CD from the library for the kids to listen to on a long road trip, and when we returned home, I was inspired to reread the whole series. And amazingly, it was full of food! If not for Heshy getting that audiobook, I would never have taken that fateful second look at The Chronicles of Narnia. Also, he rushed home from work during that last frantic week before my deadline to get that dang cork out of the bottle of wine I needed for a recipe I was testing. And I could go on, but I would probably need a second book to detail all the help and support he's given me.

By far the most important contributor to this book is Chef Chris Koch. He developed all the recipes I could not test due to my kosher diet, plus all the recipes that I technically could test but whose ingredients are impossible to find in the kosher market (like venison and game birds). Some twenty-odd recipes for this book come from this wonderfully creative chef.

Many thanks to my agent, Jason Ashlock. Jason cares not only about finding the best publishers for his clients but also about helping them expand their careers and grow as authors. I'm learning a lot from Jason, and I just love his energy and enthusiasm.

Thanks also to my team of editors, Kelly Barrales-Saylor, Regan Fisher, Kristin Zelazko, Aubrey Poole, Rachel Edwards, and Steve Geck. Their care and thoroughness in editing the manuscript ensured the best possible result—and taught me a lot about writing.

Thanks to Chef Mike Gershkovich of Mike's Bistro on the Upper West Side of Manhattan for answering my questions, and to Chef Peter Greweling of the Culinary Institute of America for helping me find an accurate candy thermometer. Finally, I'm getting consistent results with my candy making! Thanks also to food expert Harold McGee for sending me important information in response to my inquiries.

I am grateful beyond words to J. K. Rowling. Her work inspired me to write my first cookbook and to continue a career as a literary cookbook author. I am also grateful to C. S. Lewis, whose enchanting series serves as the inspiration for this book.

How many ways can you say "thank you"? I need a thesaurus here! In no order of importance, I thank Ayala and Israel Tarshish, Jack Polatsek, Abe and K. K. Polatsek, Elchanan and Annette Frankenthal, Cheryl Albert, Yaffa and Yakov Yermish, Yitz and Frimi Levi, my friends and neighbors for their enthusiastic tasting, and the engineers at Aterrasys.

I must not neglect to mention my mother for her encouragement, and for telling anyone and everyone willing to listen about her daughter, the author; my father for teaching me moral clarity, a lesson I hope I am learning well; and my parents-in-law for their unconditional love and support. I would like to list my siblings and their spouses for their love and support and for spreading the word about my books (free publicity and all that), but I'll go over my word count, God bless them! Sibs, you know who you are.

And of course, my children, Elisheva, Sarah, Eliyahu, and Toby, whose honest opinions led to better results with the recipes of which you, the reader, will enjoy the fruits.

INTRODUCTION

C. S. Lewis wrote, "Eating and reading are two pleasures that combine admirably." He also said, "You can never get a cup of tea large enough or a book long enough to suit me." Don't you just love this guy? He's a kindred spirit with those of us whose favorite pastimes are eating and reading. Lewis once said that he wrote a lot about food not because he thought that was what kids wanted to read about but because he just liked lots of good eating himself. Yes, you really could just love this guy. (By the way, C. S. stands for Clive Staples, so it's no wonder his friends called him Jack.)

I like lots of good eating myself, and also lots of good cooking. My greatest love, though, was—and still is—reading good books. I was enchanted by such classics as *Little Women*, *Little House on the Prairie*, and *Five Children and It*. The concept of afternoon tea in these old-fashioned books captured my imagination, and I longed to revive this delightful custom. I used to daydream about having tea with my friends, with my little pinkie sticking out and eating small cookies.

When I started reading the Harry Potter books as an adult, my fascination with the quaint, old-fashioned foods and customs that still survive today in Great Britain only increased. During the period that I was writing *The Unofficial Harry Potter Cookbook*, I discovered The Chronicles of Narnia series. Somehow this classic series had passed me by when I was little, and now my oldest daughter was reading them. I fell in love. Puddleglum the Marsh-wiggle. Trumpkin the Dwarf. Tumnus the Faun. But best of all, the food.

Lewis wrote with obvious relish about the food his characters ate. He didn't leave it to his readers to imagine what Lucy had for tea with Tumnus or what the magician fed her for lunch; instead, he listed every food with loving detail. We know exactly what the Pevensies took with them on their journeys and what they foraged for on the way. We learn some good lessons in cooking from Centaurs and Fauns and even Calormenes.

It's hard to pick a favorite food scene. The scenes with Puddleglum, who is absolutely certain the children will hate his food, are unforgettable. When they protest that his eel stew is delicious, he is sure then that it will disagree with them. Lasaraleen makes you want to laugh as she drives Aravis frantic over the sumptuous snacks Lasaraleen commands the slaves serve. You also can't help wishing you could eat some of those whipped cream and fruit jelly dishes while you're laughing.

In Narnia, whenever the characters eat something, you can feel their relief, comfort, or delight. Relief, warmth, and comfort when they sit down, cold and starving, to a hot dinner in the Beavers' home (*The Lion, the Witch and the Wardrobe*, chapter 7). Joy and delight at the end of their quest with a feast in Cair Paravel (*The Lion, the Witch and the Wardrobe*, chapter 17). Food isn't just something mentioned as an aside to remind us that the characters are real people. Food is almost its own character and it brings along these big emotions. When King Tirian is tied up for the night, starving, the Mice, Rabbit, and Moles bring him food, and we rejoice with him that he hasn't been forgotten; we're also moved that he still has friends willing to risk their lives to bring him sustenance (*The Last Battle*, chapter 4).

Wouldn't you love to sample some of the food you've read about? Doesn't it all sound so mouth-wateringly good? Imagine how nice it would be to sit in a cozy cave, with a fire flickering in the fireplace, and have tea with Tumnus. Few things are more pleasant than a nice chat with friends over steaming mugs of tea, washing down tender soft-boiled eggs with three kinds of toast and a sugar-dusted tea cake.

With this book, you can stop imagining and start living. Create entire meals from your favorite scenes in Narnia by following the menu plans, which cluster together recipes from each food scene. If you want to enact the feast in Cair Paravel, you don't have to look up which foods were eaten at the feast and then find each recipe individually in this book. All that work has been done for you. Simply find the feast at Cair Paravel in chapter 4, and recipes for all the foods eaten there are laid out in front of you. The recipes are graded according to ease or difficulty of preparation. A grade of 1 spoon means easy, a grade of 2 spoons means middle of the road, and a grade of 3 spoons means difficult. So you can decide what kind of challenge you're up for before entering the kitchen.

Best wishes for good cooking and happy eating!

SOME CAVEATS: MOMS AND DADS TAKE NOTE!

In this book I aimed to produce recipes for every single food reference I could glean from The Chronicles of Narnia. To remain true to the series, I included recipes for foods that you, the parents, may feel are not appropriate for children to prepare, either because the technique is too complex or the method too dangerous, or because the ingredients contain alcohol. Please use your discretion in allowing your children to create or sample them. I've included them for adult fans to enjoy.

The two main concerns you might have pertain to ingredients and method. Some recipes specify alcoholic ingredients. Where possible, I suggest substitutions. Where no substitutions are available, you decide whether a particular recipe has too much for your child to consume. Please note that many of the recipes require long cooking times, which will decrease the alcohol content. Some of the menus suggest wine or beer as an accompaniment because C. S. Lewis listed it as part of the meal. In such cases I've included substitutions for kids. Also, some of the beverages call for coffee. If you are concerned about your child drinking coffee, you can use decaf as an alternative.

Some of the methods in the recipe preparation are dangerous. Children should not attempt any recipes that require boiling sugar or deep frying. Instead they can beg you—and I back them!—to prepare these recipes for them. Young teens can cook with these techniques under close adult supervision at their parents' discretion.

I don't think I need to caution you about supervising children handling knives or working near the stove top and a hot oven, but my editor thinks I do, so I have to put that in. Having said that, I wish you fun in the kitchen and happy eating!

CHAPTER ONE
BEAUTIFUL BREAKFASTS

In our world, breakfast is said to be the most important meal of the day. We're advised to eat a healthy breakfast to give us energy and more brain power. In Narnia, breakfast is no less important, although it's certainly a far cry from the typical cereal-and-milk or toast-and-butter breakfasts we hastily swallow before heading off to school or work. After all, few of us wake up to discover that not only has a toffee tree sprouted in our backyard overnight, but that's also all there is for breakfast. But wouldn't it be interesting to try it, for a change?

I wouldn't recommend that you eat the toffee fruit first thing in the morning on an empty stomach, but the rest of the breakfast menus in this chapter provide delicious, warm, satisfying, and hearty meals for a great start to your day. And if you ever have a Centaur over for breakfast, at least you'll know what to serve his man-stomach.

BREAKFAST WITH FLEDGE

· Toffee Fruit ·

Digory is so eager to prove himself that he takes off with Polly without a thought for provisions. So the children share between them a bag of toffees, and on an impulse, Digory plants the last toffee. And lo! In the morning, they find that a toffee tree covered with soft toffee fruit has sprung up. (*The Magician's Nephew*, chapters 12–13).

TOFFEE FRUIT

Real toffee is made by boiling butter, sugar, and other ingredients to 300°F. To make a softer version, this recipe calls for boiling similar ingredients to a much lower temperature. The result is really fudge, which then has to be stirred to get that soft, melt-in-your mouth texture. The butter flavoring gives the candy a more toffee-like flavor.

2 cups dark brown sugar
2 cups whole milk
½ cup heavy cream
2 tablespoons light corn syrup
⅛ teaspoon salt

¼ teaspoon cream of tartar
1½ teaspoons pure vanilla extract
1½ teaspoons butter flavoring,
  optional

1. Place the brown sugar, milk, heavy cream, corn syrup, salt, and cream of tartar in a large saucepan (use at least a 4-quart pan to allow the mixture to expand). Bring to a boil while stirring constantly. The mixture will appear curdled but will smooth out as it cooks. Wash down the sides of the pan with a pastry brush dipped in hot water and clip a candy thermometer to the side of the pan.

2. Cook over medium-high heat, stirring constantly, until the mixture reaches 238°F, about 30 minutes. Remove the pan from the heat immediately. Continue stirring until the temperature drops to 236°F, then set aside and cool to 120°F.

3. Add the vanilla and butter flavoring, if using, and stir vigorously with a wooden spoon until the mixture turns opaque and crumbly. Scrape the mixture onto a piece of plastic wrap, cover completely, and knead gently for a few minutes to soften it.

4. Using a small cookie scoop or your fingers, scoop out or pinch off 1½-inch pieces of the mixture, keeping it covered as you work to prevent it from drying out. Roll the pieces into small logs to resemble dates and lay them on a sheet of parchment.

5. Transfer the toffee fruit to an airtight container. The candies will keep, stored properly, for several weeks, though they'll never last that long.

Makes about 30 fruits

SHASTA ON THE RUN

· Meat Pasty · Dried Figs · Green Cheese · Grape Juice ·

Shasta overhears the wealthy Tarkaan haggling with the fisherman he lives with over the price of a good, strong boy. Shasta wonders aloud if he might have a better life with the nobleman and is startled out of his wits when the rich man's horse warns him that he'd be better off dead and that he'd better run away—with the horse, of course. The two set off together, and at mealtime, Shasta is delighted to find a meat pasty and other food in the Tarkaan's saddlebag (*The Horse and His Boy*, chapter 2).

···⊰[MEAT PASTIES ♪♪♪]⊱···

Meat pasties, small handheld pies, are a convenient travel food, and English housewives used to send them with their husbands to work. This particular version is based on Mediterranean-style meat pies because the Calormenes seem to reflect that type of region and lifestyle. Dried figs and cheese also travel well, so if you want a Calormene picnic, this is the menu to bring along.

CRUST

3 cups all-purpose flour

1 tablespoon or 1 packet instant
   yeast

1 teaspoon salt

¼ cup olive oil

1 cup warm water

FILLING

2 tablespoons vegetable oil

1 medium onion, chopped

1 pound ground lamb or beef

2 cloves garlic, minced

2 tablespoons tomato paste

⅓ cup pine nuts

¼ teaspoon ground cardamom or
   cinnamon

½ teaspoon grated fresh ginger,
   optional

1 tablespoon lemon juice

1. To prepare the crust, place the flour, yeast, and salt in a mixing bowl and whisk to combine. Add the oil and water and mix well. Knead for 10 minutes, until the dough is smooth and elastic. (You can also use an electric mixer with a dough hook instead.) Add more flour 1 tablespoon at a time if the dough is sticky.

2. Lightly grease a separate mixing bowl with vegetable oil. Place the dough in the oiled bowl, turning the dough to coat it with oil on all sides. Cover the bowl with plastic wrap and set it aside in a warm, draft-free area to rise until doubled in size, 1½ to 2 hours.

3. To prepare the filling, heat the oil in a large skillet. Add the onion and cook over medium-high heat, stirring occasionally, until the onions are browned. In a large mixing bowl, combine the sautéed onion with the remaining filling ingredients. Mix well.

4. To assemble the pasties, preheat the oven to 350°F and line a baking sheet with parchment paper. Turn the dough out onto a floured work surface and divide it into 12 equal portions. Roll out the portions into 6-inch circles. Place a generous amount of filling in the centers of 6 of the dough circles, and spread the filling to within an inch of the borders. Wet the edges of the dough with water, place the remaining circles on top, and press down with your fingers to seal. Tuck the edges under to make neat circles and cut about 4 half-inch slits on top to vent.

5. Place the pasties on the prepared baking sheet and bake 40 to 50 minutes, rotating the pan halfway through baking, until the pasties are lightly browned and firm and juices are bubbling out. Allow to rest for 10 minutes before serving.

Makes 6 pasties

·•୬[Dried Figs, Green Cheese, and Grape Juice]୧•·

Green cheese is a Cheddar cheese flavored with veins of sage. Make sure to pack that along with plump, chewy figs and a bottle of grape juice (or wine, if you're a grown-up) for your picnic.

Breakfast with the Hermit

· Stick-to-Your-Ribs Oat Porridge and Cream ·

The Hermit sends Shasta on his way with the warning to run, run, run without stopping, and then turns his attention to his other visitors. Aravis has had a lion rake its claws across her back, but luckily the scratches are not deep, and within a couple of days, she's eating a hearty breakfast of porridge (*The Horse and His Boy*, chapter 11).

STICK-TO-YOUR-RIBS OAT PORRIDGE and CREAM

The ultimate healthy breakfast and comfort food, oat porridge has been eaten for breakfast for millennia and is still a popular breakfast food in Scotland. It takes a good half hour to cook, so make sure you get up extra early to prepare this breakfast—or save it for a day off.

4 cups whole or low-fat milk
1 cup steel-cut oats

Heavy cream, for serving
Honey or golden syrup, for serving

1. Bring the milk to a boil in a medium saucepan. Add the oats and stir. Cover and cook at a low simmer, stirring occasionally, until thickened, about 30 minutes.
2. Divide among 6 bowls. Serve with cream and honey or golden syrup.

Serves 6

Shasta's Breakfast with Duffle the Dwarf and His Brothers

· *Bacon, Eggs, and Mushrooms* ·

· *Porridge and Cream (Old-Fashioned Wheat Porridge)* ·

· *Toast and Butter* · *Spiced Brown Sugar Coffee* ·

Shasta has just delivered an urgent message to the strange creatures of Archenland: Prince Rabadash of Calormen is rapidly approaching with a host two hundred strong to capture Archenland and thereby expand the Calormene kingdom. Shasta hasn't eaten since yesterday, and he nearly faints with hunger when Duffle the Dwarf rescues him and orders his brothers to serve Shasta a huge and delicious breakfast (*The Horse and His Boy*, chapter 12).

This may sound like a really big breakfast, but the traditional English breakfast is even bigger. It may also include such items as beans, fried tomatoes, black pudding, and kippers, a type of cold-smoked herring. Fortunately for their waists, today most Brits stick to the modern cereal-and-milk or muffin-and-coffee style of breakfast.

Bacon, Eggs, and Mushrooms

THANKS TO CHEF CHRIS KOCH FOR THIS RECIPE.

This is a typical fry-up, a British way of preparing a meal in which various foods are fried in a pan one after the other (or all at once, why not?) and usually served for breakfast.

12 ounces sliced bacon

1 pound white button mushrooms

12 eggs

¼ cup water or milk, optional

½ teaspoon salt

¾ teaspoon ground white pepper

1. Place a 10-inch cast-iron skillet or sauté pan over medium-high heat. While the pan heats, dice the bacon into ½-inch pieces. Add to the pan and cook, stirring as needed, until the desired degree of crispness is achieved, 5 to 10 minutes.

2. While the bacon cooks, quarter the mushrooms. Remove the bacon with a slotted spoon and set on a paper towel–lined plate to drain some of the excess grease. Add the quartered mushrooms to the remaining bacon drippings in the pan and stir to coat. Cook the mushrooms for about 5 minutes or until soft.

3. Meanwhile, break the eggs into a bowl. Add the water or milk, if using. Season with salt and pepper, or as desired, and whisk until evenly blended.

4. When the mushrooms are softened, add the bacon back into the pan and stir. Reduce the heat and add the beaten eggs to the pan, stirring frequently with a wooden spoon until the eggs are just set and soft and creamy. Remove from the heat when fully cooked but still moist and serve at once on heated plates.

5. Serve with toast and butter.

Serves 4

·⊰[TOAST AND BUTTER]⊱·

You don't need a recipe for this, but C. S. Lewis mentions it as part of this great meal. It's the obvious accompaniment, for example, to the above recipe.

·⊰[PORRIDGE AND CREAM
(OLD-FASHIONED WHEAT PORRIDGE)]⊱·

Did you know that the word *cereal* derives from the Roman agriculture goddess Ceres? Both *corn* and *cereal* are general words that mean grains. Wheat is one of the oldest cultivated cereals, and crushing it and cooking it is also one of the oldest ways to prepare it.

1 ¼ cups crushed wheat, such as
    Wheatena
3 ½ cups whole or low-fat milk

Pinch salt
Heavy cream and honey, for serving

If crushed wheat is too wheaty for you, cook 4 cups milk with ½ cup farina cereal, like Cream of Wheat, in a saucepan over medium-high heat. Add ¼ cup brown sugar, 1 teaspoon cinnamon, and a pinch of salt. Cook, stirring occassionally, until bubbles form on the sides, about 5 minutes. Continue cooking, stirring constantly, until thickened and bubbly, another 3 to 4 minutes. Pour the heavy cream over the porridge, but omit the honey for serving.

1. Combine the crushed wheat, milk, and salt in a saucepan and cook over medium-high heat, stirring occasionally, until bubbles form on the sides, about 5 minutes. Continue cooking, stirring constantly, until thickened and bubbly, another 3 to 4 minutes.

2. Divide into 4 bowls. Pour the heavy cream and honey over the porridge before serving.

Serves 4

·⊰[SPICED BROWN SUGAR COFFEE ♪♪♪]⊱·

Though tea is the national drink in England, coffeehouses became popular too in the mid-seventeenth century. Coffee arrived in Europe from the Middle East, and a Turkish Jew named Jacob is credited with opening the first coffeehouse in England.

1 mug hot brewed coffee, regular or
   decaf
1 tablespoon brown sugar

Pinch ground nutmeg
Pinch ground allspice
Heavy cream, to taste

1. Add the sugar and spices to the mug of coffee and stir to combine. Add the heavy cream.

Serves 1

Breakfast with Trumpkin the Dwarf

· Fire-Roasted Pavenders (Fried Rainbow Smelts) · Tree-Ripe Apples ·

· Crystal Well Water ·

Once again, the Pevensies find themselves in Narnia, and before they know it, they are busy rescuing a dwarf from a couple of evil Telmarines. Naturally, the Pevensies share a meal with Trumpkin the Dwarf, who helps them prepare a more satisfying meal than the apples they've been living on (*Prince Caspian*, chapter 3).

·⊰[Fire-Roasted Pavenders (Fried Rainbow Smelts) ♪♪♪]⊱·

THANKS TO CHEF CHRIS KOCH FOR THIS RECIPE.

Pavenders are rainbow-colored fish that are unfortunately found only in Narnia, so we ordinary humans must make do with rainbow smelts (though any other kind of smelt will also do). Smelt is also called candlefish because it's so high in fat that if you dry it out and string a wick through it, it will burn like a candle. Don't let that put you off eating it, though. It's really quite delicious!

2 pounds rainbow smelt, or other type of smelt if rainbow is not available	*2 cups all-purpose flour* *Vegetable oil for frying*

1. Place half of the smelt inside a resealable bag. Seal the bag and pound it with a skillet or other large flat-bottomed pan. Don't pound too hard, though—just enough until the fish is flattened. Remove the smelt from the bag and pat the smelt dry with paper towels. Repeat with the remaining smelt.

2. Place the flour in the bag. Place the fish in the bag and shake to coat it evenly with the flour.

3. Heat ½ inch oil in a large skillet over medium heat until a bit of flour bubbles when placed in the pan. Place the smelt in the pan a few at a time and fry until golden brown, 2 to 3 minutes per side. Drain on paper towels.

Serves 4

ᢟ Tree-Ripe Apples ᢟ

Enjoy the Fire-Roasted Pavenders with crisp apples for dessert. I recommend a sweet-tart apple such as Honeycrisp, or a sweet apple such as Gala.

ᢟ Crystal Well-Water ᢟ

Wash the meal down with fresh ice water.

FOOD SENT BY ASLAN

· Fire–Roasted Fish (Broiled Kippers) ·

Oh, it's hard to say good-bye! When it's time for Edmund, Lucy, and Eustace to leave Narnia after their adventures on the Dawn Treader, Aslan, in the form of a lamb, sends them off with a delicious breakfast of roasted fish (*The Voyage of the Dawn Treader*, chapter 16).

··ɔ] FIRE-ROASTED FISH (BROILED KIPPERS) ♪♪♪ [ɔ··

Eating kippers for breakfast is very traditional in England, but they are hard to find in the United States. You can order them online from UK-based companies for a price.

8 kippers
2 tablespoons melted butter, for brushing over the kippers

Salt, to taste
Freshly ground black pepper, to taste, for sprinkling

1. Broil the kippers on high for 5 minutes until crisp.
2. Brush butter over the kippers, then sprinkle with the salt and pepper.
3. Serve with toast.

Serves 4

Food from a Faun

· Cheesy Scrambled Eggs · Hot Buttered Toast ·

· Sweet and Crunchy Cinnamon Toast ·

Jill and Eustace have finally escaped the terrifying Underworld and are grateful to eat the scrambled eggs and toast that Orruns the Faun has prepared for them for breakfast the next morning (*The Silver Chair*, chapter 16).

⌐ CHEESY SCRAMBLED EGGS ⌐

Eggs are a wonder food. I can't help wondering how someone discovered that you can beat the whites into a snowy mound or that you can use the yolks to thicken custard. You can also prepare them in many ways for breakfast or enrich and leaven cakes with them. The uses for eggs are almost endless. But aside from their usefulness, eggs were also revered all over the world: in many cultures from Europe to the Middle East, for thousands of years, eggs have symbolized fertility and rebirth.

1 tablespoon butter	*Salt, to taste*
8 large eggs	*Freshly ground black pepper, to taste*
¼ cup heavy cream	*1 cup shredded mild Cheddar cheese*

1. Heat the butter in a large skillet over low heat. While the butter is melting, whisk together the eggs, heavy cream, and salt and pepper. Whisk in the cheese and pour the mixture into the skillet. Cook over medium-low heat, stirring and scraping constantly with a wooden spoon, until set, 5 to 7 minutes. Serve immediately.

Serves 4

⊶❁ HOT BUTTERED TOAST ❁⊷

Toast goes a long way back. In the Middle Ages, people toasted bread in order to better sop up liquid from stews; this dish was actually called *sops*. Later cookbooks such as *Mrs. Beeton's Book of Household Management* (1861) gave careful instructions for toasting bread ("Cut as many nice even slices as may be required, rather more than ¼ inch in thickness, and toast them before a very bright fire...and send the toast quickly to table"). This cookbook also described how to cut the toast into pieces after it's been buttered, and the author recommended that readers use the best quality butter. Of course, toast must be served immediately, as it becomes tough when cold.

Luckily, with toasters and toaster ovens that can be set to light, medium, and dark, instructions for making buttered toast are totally unnecessary. With minimum fuss and bother, you can serve a platter of it every time you make Orruns's breakfast.

⊶❁ SWEET AND CRUNCHY CINNAMON TOAST 🥄🥄🥄 ❁⊷

In the 1600s cinnamon toast was made by spreading a paste of sugar, cinnamon, and wine over toast. This nonalcoholic version is super easy, as easy as buttered toast.

*8 slices good-quality sandwich bread,
    for toasting*
Softened butter, for serving

¼ cup sugar
1 teaspoon ground cinnamon

1. Toast the bread to the desired doneness and spread with the butter. While the bread is toasting, mix the sugar and cinnamon together.
2. Sprinkle the cinnamon sugar over the toast.

Serves 4

> For an extra-delicious crunch, use turbinado sugar in place of the granulated sugar.

Breakfast for the Man-Stomach of Centaurs

· Stick-to-Your-Ribs Porridge (Old-Fashioned Oat Porridge) ·

· Pavenders (Batter-Dipped Rainbow Smelts) · Fried Kidneys ·

· Crispy Bacon · Tender Omelet with Sautéed Vegetable Filling ·

· Baked York Ham · Toast with Sweet Orange Marmalade ·

· Coffee and Beer, with Ginger Beer for the Kids ·

That's a huge breakfast! Orruns tells Eustace to slow down on his scrambled eggs and toast; there's no need to hurry. The Centaurs they're waiting for take a long time to eat their meals because they have two stomachs. First they feed their man-stomach; then they feed their horse-stomach. Be sure to have this menu handy next time a Centaur comes calling (*The Silver Chair*, chapter 16).

This breakfast, huge as it sounds, is actually quite similar to the very large traditional breakfast that the upper and middle classes in Europe once enjoyed. Such a breakfast often included, in one meal, porridge with cream and honey or treacle (golden syrup), toast, fried bacon, fried kidneys, fried mushrooms, fried tomatoes, and fried eggs. This breakfast is appropriately called a *fry-up*. After you prepare this meal, make sure to serve it with a large pot of coffee, beer for the grown-ups, and ginger beer for the kids.

··❧ STICK-TO-YOUR-RIBS PORRIDGE (OLD-FASHIONED OAT PORRIDGE) ❧··

The traditional way to eat this porridge in Scotland is to dip each hot spoonful into cold milk or cream and eat it unsweetened. On the other hand, the British have a very important tradition, which should be religiously upheld, of adding lots of sugar or treacle to their porridge. Use the Stick-to-Your-Ribs Oat Porridge and Cream recipe on page 11 to prepare this hearty dish.

⋅⋅◦] PAVENDERS (BATTER-DIPPED RAINBOW SMELTS) 🥄🥄🥄 [◦⋅⋅

Because pavenders are unavailable in our world, Chef Chris Koch has generously shared his recipe for beer-battered fried rainbow smelts.

⅔ cup all-purpose flour

½ teaspoon baking powder

½ teaspoon salt

⅛ teaspoon white pepper

*1½ tablespoons beaten egg (beat a
    whole egg and measure out the
    correct amount)*

½ cup beer, or club soda if desired

Flour, as needed, for dredging

Vegetable oil for frying

*2 pounds whole rainbow smelt, or
    other smelt if rainbow is not
    available*

1. Sift the flour, baking powder, salt, and pepper together. Beat the egg in a separate bowl. Add the beer to the beaten egg. Add the egg-and-beer mixture to the dry ingredients; mix until smooth.

2. Rinse the smelt and pat dry.

3. Heat 1 inch oil in a pot at least 4 inches deep or in an automatic fryer to 350°F or until the oil bubbles immediately when you drop in a bit of batter. When the oil is hot enough, place the flour in a plastic bag. Add as many smelt as fit loosely in the bag and toss to coat with flour.

4. Gather 3 or 4 smelt by the tail end. Dip into the batter and carefully drop into the hot oil. Repeat a couple of times, but don't crowd the pan. There should be some space between each smelt in the oil. Cook, turning as needed, for 3 minutes or until golden brown. Transfer to paper towels to drain and repeat until all the fish has been fried.

> To check if the oil is hot enough without a thermometer, drop a piece of bread into the oil. It should bubble up immediately but not turn brown right away

Serves 4

·⊃[Fried Kidneys 🥄🥄🥄]ϲ·

THANKS TO CHEF CHRIS KOCH FOR THIS RECIPE.

Kidneys are not very popular in the United States because of their particular function in animals. It is the same as their role in humans, and if you were listening in your biology class, you know what that is: removing waste from the blood stream as urine. The rest of the world, however, has no problem with this, and people often enjoy kidneys in England for breakfast. The most popular kidneys come from sheep (mutton and lamb) or calves. The kidneys should be cooked quickly so that they don't harden.

4 kidneys	*8 slices bread, toasted*
9 tablespoons (½ cup plus 1	*Salt, to taste*
tablespoon) butter, divided	*Freshly ground black pepper, to taste*

1. Clean the kidneys by splitting each kidney lengthwise, exposing the fat and sinew. Remove the fat, and again slice each kidney in half lengthwise, to a thickness of ¼ inch.

2. Heat a skillet or sauté pan over high heat and add 8 tablespoons butter to the pan.

3. When the butter is melted, lay the kidney slices in the pan and fry them for 3 minutes. Check if they are brown. If not, fry another 2 minutes; then fry on the other side for the same amount of time. There should be a sizzle at all times. Be careful of the heat—if it is too high the kidneys will burn.

4. Allow 2 pieces of dry toast per person. Place the cooked kidneys on the toast and season with salt and pepper. Using the remaining tablespoon butter, place a small piece on each kidney and pour the gravy from the pan over the kidneys and toast. Serve very hot.

Serves 4

⋅≼[crispy bacon 🥄🥄🥄]≽⋅

THANKS TO CHEF CHRIS KOCH FOR THIS RECIPE.

In olden times, almost everyone kept pigs (they cost nothing to maintain because they could forage for scraps), and even the poor were able to include bacon in their diets. In England, thin slices of bacon are called rashers. Following are two methods for cooking bacon. The first is the easiest, producing flat, even strips, but the second is faster and doesn't require preheating the oven.

1 pound smoked bacon, sliced

METHOD 1

1. Preheat the oven to 400°F. Line a rimmed baking tray with aluminum foil. (This will help make cleanup easier.)
2. Lay the strips of bacon in one layer, slightly overlapping the edges. Place the tray of bacon in the oven and cook for 15 minutes or until the bacon reaches the desired degree of doneness.
3. With a pair of tongs, transfer the bacon to paper towels to drain. Drain the fat from the baking tray into a heat-proof container and refrigerate, reserving it for later uses, such as frying onions to add to a dish for a smoky, meaty flavor. Carefully remove the foil and discard.

METHOD 2

1. Place a heavy skillet or sauté pan over medium-high heat. Lay the bacon in the pan. Cook until the edges begin to brown, turn the strips over, and cook until the desired degree of crispness is achieved, turning as needed.
2. Using this pan method, the strips will curl and shrink. If you have a bacon press, place it on top of the strips while they cook. Transfer the bacon to paper towels to drain.

Serves 6

⌐I TENDER OMELET WITH SAUTÉED VEGETABLE FILLING ♪♪♪ I⌐

Need anything more be said about eggs? Well, actually, yes! People used to think that eggshells have medicinal value, and an ancient recipe calls for storing eggs in a jar with lemon and rum until the eggshells completely dissolve, then drinking some of the liquid every day to restore health and strength. Not to worry: the following recipe contains no eggshells (unless you're careless when you crack 'em).

FILLING

3 tablespoons vegetable oil	1 celery rib, chopped
1 onion, chopped	½ teaspoon dried marjoram, optional
10 ounces mushrooms, sliced	½ teaspoon dried tarragon, optional
½ green pepper, chopped	Salt, to taste
½ red pepper, chopped	Freshly ground black pepper, to taste

OMELET

1 teaspoon butter	Salt, to taste
8 large eggs	Freshly ground black pepper, to taste

1. To prepare the filling, heat the oil in a large skillet and add all the remaining filling ingredients. Cook over medium-high heat, stirring occasionally with a wooden spoon, until the water cooks out and the vegetables are browned, about 20 minutes. Set aside.

2. Heat the butter in a 12-inch nonstick skillet. Working with 2 eggs at a time,

> You can use any herbs you want in place of the marjoram and tarragon, such as parsley and dill.

beat the eggs with salt and pepper and pour into the pan. Swirl the pan to distribute the egg evenly over the surface. Cook until the eggs are set, then slide the omelet onto a plate. Place a quarter of the filling on one side and fold over. Repeat with the remaining eggs.

Serves 4

·ᵓ꒐ baked York ham ♪♪♪ ꒐ᵓ·

THANKS TO CHEF CHRIS KOCH FOR THIS RECIPE.

This recipe for clove-studded ham reflects the classic British preparation of cooked ham. York ham refers to the method of curing the ham, which is different from the smoked hams found in your typical grocery store. York ham has a lighter color and milder flavor.

1 (12- to 14-pound) York ham (substitute smoked country ham such as Smithfield, if necessary)	*1 tablespoon whole cloves*
	2 tablespoons English mustard
	2 tablespoons brown sugar
1½ cups ale	*2 tablespoons honey*

1. Place the ham in a pot large enough to hold it or in an insulated cooler. Cover completely with cold water and place in a cool place. Drain and refill the water every 8 hours for a total of 48 hours.

2. Preheat the oven to 425°F. Line a large roasting pan with foil extending 12 inches over each side. Remove the ham from the water and place it in the middle of the foil-lined pan. Pour the ale over the ham, and then completely enclose the ham in the foil to create a tent effect. The foil should be tightly sealed but with room for air to circulate around the ham. Bake 3½ to 4 hours for a 12-pound ham.

3. Thirty minutes before the end of the cooking time, remove the ham from the oven. With potholders or oven mitts, carefully open the foil tent. Take the skin off the ham, leaving behind as much fat as you can. Score the fat in a diamond pattern with a sharp knife (run the knife down the ham in a series of diagonal lines from top to bottom, and then create diagonal lines running the opposite direction to create the diamond effect). Stud the center of each diamond with a clove.

4. Combine the English mustard, brown sugar, and honey in a bowl to make a glaze. Brush the glaze over the ham. Return the ham to the oven, reduce the temperature to 350°F, and cook uncovered for 30 minutes longer.

5. When the ham is done, remove it from the oven and let it rest for 15 minutes. Slice the ham and transfer it to a large platter. Drizzle the cooking liquid over the ham and serve.

Serves 24

·◌[TOAST WITH SWEET ORANGE MARMALADE ⌇⌇⌇]◌·

Marmalade was originally solid and didn't become jellylike and spreadable until the eighteenth century. It was served as a candy and even used in medicine. The Scots are credited with creating marmalade as we know it. Marmalade is supposed to be made from the bitter Seville oranges, but you can use the typical sweet oranges specified in this recipe.

4 navel oranges   *2 cups sugar*
Juice of 1 lemon

I. Peel the oranges with a sharp vegetable peeler to remove the zest in strips. Chop the strips finely and place in a small saucepan with water to cover. Bring to a boil and simmer over medium-low heat for 2 hours. Strain the zest through a fine-mesh sieve and rinse with cold water. Drain.

2. Juice the oranges and pour the juice into a 3- to 4-quart saucepan, along with the lemon juice, sugar, and orange zest. Bring to a boil while stirring constantly. Wash down the sides of the pan with a pastry brush dipped in hot water. Clip a candy thermometer to the side of the pan.

> Homemade marmalade is more intensely flavored and orangey than store-bought, but it's also more liquidy. You can use fruit pectin, found by the canning supplies in your local supermarket, to thicken the mixture. Experiment with small amounts of pectin to get the consistency you want.

3. Cook the mixture over medium-high heat, stirring frequently, until the mixture reaches 225°F. Remove from the heat and allow to cool. Pour the mixture into a jar and refrigerate. Serve with toast, of course.

Makes approximately 2 cups, or fills one 14-ounce jar

·◌[COFFEE AND BEER]◌·

Such a big breakfast needs to be washed down with something tasty and comforting, and what's more satisfying than a mug of frothy coffee (decaf for the kids)? And nothing beats ice-cold beer for a refreshing end to a heavy meal. I recommend ginger beer (recipe on page 41) for younger people.

FOOD FOR TIRIAN BROUGHT TO NARNIA FROM OUR WORLD

· Hard–Boiled Egg Sandwiches ·

· Meltingly Scrumptious Grilled Cheese Sandwiches ·

· The Best Tuna Sandwiches ·

King Tirian of Narnia is having a bad time of it. By command of the Ape, he's been tied to a tree and left there all night. He wakes from a vision of the Seven Friends of Narnia to find that he is cold and wet and stiff. Luckily, the vision was real, and the Seven Friends now know he's in trouble. They immediately send Jill and Eustace to set him free and feed him a large breakfast (*The Last Battle*, chapter 5).

⋅ᵅ] HarD–BOILED EGG SanDWICHES ///[ᵒ⋅⋅

Yet another great use for eggs!

*4 large hard-boiled eggs, peeled
 and mashed*

2 tablespoons mayonnaise

1 tablespoon finely chopped scallion

Salt, to taste

Freshly ground black pepper, to taste

*1 or 2 thinly sliced medium
 cucumbers, for serving*

4 slices good-quality sandwich bread

1. Mix the eggs with the mayonnaise, scallion, and salt and pepper.
2. Layer the thinly sliced cucumbers on each of two slices of bread. Spread half the egg mixture over each cucumber-lined slice and cover with the remaining slices.
3. Cut the sandwiches diagonally in half to form triangles and serve at once. (If left for too long, the bread will become soggy from the cucumbers.)

Serves 2

MELTINGLY SCRUMPTIOUS GRILLED CHEESE SANDWICHES

A favorite of kids everywhere, and one very hungry king.

4 slices good-quality sandwich bread
Butter
English mustard

1 cup sliced mushrooms
1 cup shredded mild Cheddar cheese

1. Heat a large skillet over medium heat. Butter the 4 slices of bread on one side only and lay them out on a plate, butter side down. Spread the English mustard on 2 of the slices. Divide the mushrooms between the 2 slices, then divide the cheese and spread over the mushrooms. Top with the remaining slices of bread, butter side up.

2. Transfer the two sandwiches to the skillet and press down with a spatula. When the bread is crisp and golden, after about 5 minutes, flip the sandwiches over and cook until that side is crisp and golden, too. Transfer to a dinner plate and slice in half diagonally to form triangles.

Serves 2

THE BEST TUNA SANDWICHES

The third kind of sandwich the children bring Tirian is filled with a paste that he doesn't recognize, as it isn't eaten in Narnia. He eats it because he's hungry, but he doesn't much care for it. It could have been peanut butter. Or it could have been tuna. Your guess is as good as mine! But I suspect that if it had been a tuna sandwich made using my husband Heshy's recipe, which follows, King Tirian would have liked it very much indeed, hungry or not.

1 (6-ounce) can white tuna, chunk
  or solid
3 tablespoons mayonnaise
½ celery rib, finely chopped
Pinch ground cayenne pepper

4 slices fresh sandwich bread
Thinly sliced tomatoes and
  iceberg or romaine lettuce
  leaves, for serving

1. Mash the tuna with the mayonnaise until combined. Add the celery and cayenne pepper and mix well.
2. Spread half the tuna mixture over each of 2 slices of bread. Layer the tomato slices and lettuce leaves over the tuna and top with the remaining slices of bread. Cut the sandwiches in half diagonally to form triangles.

Serves 2

POGGIN THE DWARF MAKES BREAKFAST

· Pigeon Stew with Wood Sorrel ·

Tirian is feeling down. The dwarfs have just gone over to the enemy, and now there's no telling how many other types of Narnians he will lose as well. But he is considerably cheered when Poggin the Dwarf joins up, having deserted his own brethren in favor of Narnia. And he proves his usefulness when he makes a pigeon stew for his hungry companions flavored with a Narnian weed similar to our common wood sorrel, though of course superior in taste and quality (*The Last Battle*, chapter 7).

PIGEON STEW WITH WOOD SORREL

Wood sorrel is also known as *alleluia* because it flowers between Easter and Pentecost, a time of great celebration. Native Americans have used wood sorrel in both food and medicine. Here in Philadelphia, my family and I have noticed that it's available from early spring to late summer. So go ahead and pick a bunch for your stew; just make sure that you wash it really well.

2 pigeons or Cornish game hens
2 tablespoons vegetable oil, if needed
1 onion, cut in half from pole to pole
*   and sliced*
10 ounces mushrooms
2 garlic cloves, minced
1 tablespoon all-purpose flour

1 cup chicken broth
1 bunch freshly picked wood sorrel,
*   cleaned and chopped (stems and*
*   flowers discarded)*
Salt, to taste
Freshly ground black pepper, to taste

1. Cut the birds in half with a chef's knife, one breast and one leg per portion. Open the pieces to flatten them out. Spray a Dutch oven or wide pot with cooking spray and sear the pieces over high heat, skin side first, two at a

time, until crusty brown on both sides, 2 to 3 minutes per side. Transfer to a large plate.

2. If very little fat has been left in the pan, add the oil. Add the onions and mushrooms and cook over medium-high heat, stirring to scrape up the flavorful browned bits on the bottom of the pot. Continue to cook, stirring occasionally, until all the water is cooked out and the mixture has browned. Add the garlic and stir just until fragrant, a few seconds. Add the flour and stir to combine. Pour in the chicken broth and stir to combine. Add the wood sorrel, salt, and pepper. Lay the pigeon pieces or Cornish hens over the sauce and simmer, covered, until tender, 1½ to 2 hours.

3. Serve, passing the sauce separately.

Serves 4

CHAPTER TWO
SNACKS, TEAS, AND MEALS ON THE RUN

One of my favorite scenes in Narnia is the cozy tea Lucy shares with Mr. Tumnus in his snug little cave. It's always been a fantasy of mine to revive the old custom of afternoon tea. There's something so quaint and delightful about pausing in the middle of the afternoon to savor a pretty teacup filled with a sweet, steaming liquid and an old-fashioned pastry to go along with it. A quiet Saturday afternoon when you have nothing to do is the perfect time to invite your friends for some tea. You can tell them to come early and help you make the scones from the "High Tea after Battle" menu on page 58. Your mom might even let you use her real china if you ask very nicely.

Tea in England goes back to about the 1600s, when it was introduced from China and quickly replaced ale as the national drink. People believed that tea was good for you, which today we know is true: teas are chock-full of immunity-boosting antioxidants. The government, suffering from a drop in the sales of alcoholic beverages, imposed such steep taxes on tea that people turned to smuggling. Clippers, which the Americans first designed and the British soon adopted, could bring tea from Asia more quickly. These impressive streamlined ships could travel almost as fast as ocean liners today.

Historians credit Anne of Bedford, a nineteenth-century duchess, with introducing the tradition of afternoon tea. In those days in aristocratic circles, dinner was often served as late as eight o'clock. The duchess noticed that by around four in the afternoon, she would begin feeling more than a bit peckish. So she invited some ladies over and they sat at the low tables in the parlor and had tea with fancy pastries.

This caught on quickly throughout the rest of the country. The working classes rolled tea and supper into one meal, which families ate at their one high dinner table (no low tables in the parlor for them!). This meal became known as high tea.

The traditional way to make tea is to pour boiling water into the teapot, swirl it around, and then pour it out. This warms the teapot and keeps the tea hot a little longer. Then put one teaspoon of loose tea and one cup of hot water per person into the pot. Add one more teaspoon of tea, "for the pot," as the Brits say. Serve with sugar cubes and milk or cream.

THE SWEETS THEY HAD IN THOSE DAYS

· Handmade Chocolate–Covered Fondant ·

· Easy Chocolate–Covered Fondant ·

· Can't–Have–Just–One Coconut Fudge Bonbons ·

· Chewy White Nougat · Easy Nougat · Ginger Beer · Rich Plum Cake ·

"In those days, if you were a boy you had to wear a stiff Eton collar every day, and schools were usually nastier than they are now. But meals were nicer; and as for sweets, I won't tell you how cheap and good they were, because it would only make your mouth water in vain" (*The Magician's Nephew*, chapter 1).

C. S. Lewis had a point. Sweets today are cheaper than he would have ever thought possible, but to eat handmade chocolate creams and bonbons, you have to pay a fortune. However, I *will* tell you about it, and your mouth *won't* water in vain—because you can make them yourself. Just make sure you have an accurate candy thermometer, and that's pretty much all the specialized equipment you need to make some good old-fashioned candy. The following sweets, though not specifically mentioned by name in the series, reflect confections of the time.

·⊰[HANDMADE CHOCOLATE-COVERED FONDANT ℓℓℓ]⊱·

I am always impressed by the ingenuity and resourcefulness of folks who invented or created substances without the benefit of modern technology and equipment. Fondant has been around since the mid-1800s, and it's a mystery to me how someone figured out that if you supersaturate sugar with water, then beat it vigorously, it will result in a creamy confection that can be used in many ways. An easier, kid-friendly chocolate-covered fondant recipe follows this one.

3 cups sugar

¼ cup corn syrup

¼ teaspoon cream of tartar

½ cup water

1½ pounds bittersweet chocolate, chopped into chunks, or 1½ pounds chocolate candy coating pieces

1. Grease an 8-inch square pan, line it with parchment paper to come up 2 sides (to form handles for easy removal), and set aside. Place the sugar, corn syrup, cream of tartar, and water in a medium saucepan and cook over medium-high heat, stirring constantly, until the sugar dissolves. Wash down the sides of the pan with a pastry brush dipped in hot water.

2. Clip a candy thermometer to the pot and cook without stirring until the thermometer registers 238°F. Remove from the heat and cool to 125°F.

3. Beat with a wooden spoon until the mixture turns white and creamy and pour it into the prepared pan. Allow it to cool until firm. If the fondant remains too soft to cut, refrigerate for 15 minutes or so to harden.

If you stirred too long and the fondant turned hard, scrape it onto a piece of plastic wrap. Wrap it loosely, and then knead the fondant, in the plastic, until smooth and pliable. Seal in a plastic bag and leave overnight. Pinch off small pieces and roll into balls before dipping into chocolate, uncovering only a bit of the fondant at a time to prevent drying.

4. While the mixture is cooling, melt the chocolate. There are many methods to properly melt chocolate. One of the easiest ways is to put the chocolate in a glass bowl and microwave on high for 30-second increments, stirring after each one. When the chocolate is almost all melted, remove the bowl from the microwave and stir until completely melted.

5. Remove the fondant from the pan using the parchment paper as handles, and place it on a cutting board. Using a sharp oiled chef's knife, make 7 cuts in both directions to form sixty-four 1-inch squares. Dip the squares in the melted chocolate and set on a parchment-lined baking sheet to set, about 5 minutes.

Makes 64 pieces

EASY CHOCOLATE-COVERED FONDANT 🥄🥄🥄

4 tablespoons (¼ cup) butter, at room
   temperature
3 cups confectioners' sugar
1 teaspoon pure vanilla extract

¼ cup light corn syrup
1 pound bittersweet chocolate,
   broken into pieces, or chocolate
   coating pieces

1. Combine all the ingredients except for the chocolate in a large mixing bowl. Using an electric mixer, mix on low speed until combined. Increase speed to medium and beat until the mixture forms a dough. Remove from the mixing bowl, shape into a disk, and wrap in plastic wrap. Store in the refrigerator until ready to use, up to 1 week.

2. Before using, bring the fondant to room temperature. Meanwhile, melt the chocolate using the steps outlined in the previous recipe. When the fondant and chocolate are ready, use a small cookie scoop or your fingers to pinch off 1½-inch pieces, roll into balls, and dip into the tempered chocolate or chocolate coating. Lay the candies on a parchment-paper-lined tray to set.

> To make peppermint creams, replace the vanilla with ¼ teaspoon peppermint extract.

Makes about 2½ dozen candies

CAN'T-HAVE-JUST-ONE COCONUT FUDGE BONBONS 🥄🥄🥄

Bonbons, a French word for candy, were popularly gifted in fancy boxes in the eighteenth and nineteenth centuries in the form of chocolate confections, fondant confections, and nut candies like pieces of nougat. Such gift boxes are still popular today, especially for holidays.

2 cups whole milk
2 cups granulated sugar
4 tablespoons (¼ cup) butter
2 tablespoons light corn syrup
¼ teaspoon salt

¼ teaspoon cream of tartar
1½ cups shredded sweetened coconut,
   finely ground
1½ teaspoons pure vanilla extract
Bowl of confectioners' sugar, for coating

1. Place the milk, sugar, butter, corn syrup, salt, and cream of tartar in a large saucepan (at least 4 quarts, to allow the mixture to expand). Bring to a boil while stirring constantly. The mixture will appear curdled but will smooth out as it cooks. Wash down the sides of the pan with a pastry brush dipped in hot water and clip a candy thermometer to the side of the pan.

2. Cook over medium-high heat, stirring constantly, until the mixture reaches 238°F, about 30 minutes. Remove from the heat immediately. Continue stirring until the temperature drops to 236°F. Set aside and cool to 120°F.

3. Add the coconut and vanilla extract and beat vigorously with a wooden spoon until the mixture turns opaque and crumbly and is impossible to stir. Scrape the mixture onto a piece of plastic wrap, cover completely with the plastic wrap, and knead gently for a few minutes to soften the mixture and form it into a smooth mass.

4. Using a small cookie scoop or your fingers, scoop out or pinch off 1½-inch pieces of the mixture. Work with a few pieces at a time, and keep the mixture covered with the plastic as you work to prevent drying out. Roll the pieces into balls, coat with confectioners' sugar, and lay them on a sheet of parchment.

5. When completely cool, transfer the coconut fudge bonbons to an airtight container. The candies will keep, stored properly, for several weeks, though they most likely won't last that long.

Makes about 2½ dozen bonbons

·⊰〚 CHEWY WHITE NOUGAT *♪♪♪* 〛⊱·

Since at least the 1700s, candymakers in Montélimar, France, have been producing this incredibly delicious candy, so much so that nougat and Montélimar are virtually synonyms. One has to wonder, how in the world did they make nougat without stand mixers? They must have had major biceps—or else they took turns beating the egg whites.

This is quite possibly the most difficult recipe in this book (barring the comfits later on), and it requires some experience with sugar boiling to properly stream the hot sugar syrup into the beating egg whites. It might take a few tries to learn when the egg whites are beaten to the correct consistency, and pouring the hot sugar syrup requires care and a steady hand. Don't let that discourage you! It's worth messing up a few times to learn how to make this wonderful confection. However, an easy-to-make version follows this one.

Cornstarch, for dusting the pan	*1½ cups corn syrup*
4 egg whites, at room temperature	*1½ cups honey*
¼ teaspoon cream of tartar	*¼ cup vegetable oil*
¼ teaspoon salt	*½ cup confectioners' sugar, sifted*
1 tablespoon pure vanilla extract	*1 cup toasted almonds*
2 cups granulated sugar, divided	*1 cup toasted unsalted pistachio nuts*
1 cup water	

1. Grease a 9-inch-by-13-inch pan and dust it with cornstarch. Before you start, be sure to have all the ingredients measured and ready to use. Place the egg whites, cream of tartar, salt, and vanilla in the large mixing bowl. Fit the mixer with the whisk attachment.

2. Combine the granulated sugar, water, corn syrup, and honey in a large sauce-pan. Cook over high heat, stirring constantly, until the sugar is dissolved, 5 to 10 minutes. Wash the sides of the pan with a pastry brush dipped in hot water and clip a candy thermometer to the side of the pan. Continue cooking until the mixture reaches 250°F. Leave on the heat.

3. While the sugar syrup continues to cook, turn the mixer onto medium-high speed and whip until the egg whites are foamy. Increase the speed to high and continue whipping until the mixture forms soft peaks. Watch the sugar mixture and remove it from the heat when it reaches 285°F, stirring occasionally to prevent scorching. Once you remove it from the heat, stir quickly and constantly until the temperature drops to 284°F (the syrup will rise a couple of degrees first, and that's okay). The sugar syrup should reach 285°F and the egg whites should reach the soft peak stage at around the same time.

The best thing to do with nougat, of course, is to dip the pieces into melted chocolate.

4. Reduce the mixer speed to medium and slowly stream the hot sugar syrup into the beating egg whites, pouring against the side of bowl. Once all the sugar syrup has been incorporated, continue whipping for 10 minutes.

5. Reduce the mixing speed to the slowest speed and slowly add the oil. The nougat

will separate and slap around the bowl, but just keep mixing until it becomes smooth again. Slowly add the confectioners' sugar. Remove the bowl from the mixer and fold in the nuts by hand.

6. Scrape the mixture into the prepared pan. Cover with parchment paper and smooth the mixture into the edges of the pan with your hands. Cool completely overnight at room temperature. Once the mixture is completely cool, the parchment paper will peel off easily.

7. Cut into pieces as desired and wrap individually in plastic wrap.

Makes 1 9-inch-by-13-inch slab

··⁌ EASY NOUGAT ⫻ ⫻ ⫻ ⁍··

4 tablespoons (¼ cup) butter, at room
    temperature
3 cups confectioners' sugar
1 teaspoon pure vanilla extract
¼ cup light corn syrup

½ cup marshmallow crème
½ cup nonfat milk powder
1 pound bittersweet chocolate,
    broken into pieces, or chocolate
    coating pieces

1. Combine all the ingredients except the chocolate in a large mixing bowl. Using an electric mixer, mix on low speed until combined. Increase the speed to medium and beat until the mixture forms a dough. Remove from the mixing bowl, shape into a disk, and wrap in plastic wrap. The nougat can be used right away or stored in the refrigerator for up to 1 week.

2. Before using, bring the nougat to room temperature. Meanwhile, melt the chocolate. Use a small cookie scoop or your fingers to pinch off 1½–inch pieces of the nougat, roll into balls, and dip into the melted chocolate or chocolate coating. Lay the candies on a parchment-paper-lined tray to set.

Makes about 3 dozen candies

GINGER BEER ♪♪♪

Polly has discovered a sort of tunnel in the attic that runs along the back of the row houses where she lives. As it's a rainy summer, she spends a lot of time there exploring, and proudly shows Digory her haunt, littered with ginger beer bottles to make it look more like a smuggler's cave (*The Magician's Nephew*, chapter 1).

When I read about this, I assumed that ginger beer was a reference to the bottled soda we know today as ginger ale. Turns out I was wrong! This British specialty is easy to make and so refreshing you'll no doubt want to take a couple of bottles with you when you go exploring.

¼ cup freshly grated ginger
Zest and juice of 2 lemons
1 cup sugar

1 cup water
⅛ teaspoon instant yeast

1. Place the ginger, lemon zest and juice, sugar, and water in a medium saucepan and bring to a boil while stirring. Remove from the heat and let steep, covered, for 1 hour.
2. Strain the mixture through a fine-mesh sieve, pushing down on the pulp to extract as much juice as possible. Funnel the mixture into a clean 2-liter bottle. Add the yeast and enough water to come up to within 2 to 3 inches of the top. Cap tightly and store at room temperature for 2 days, occasionally and gently tilting the bottle upside down to mix.
3. Chill until cold and serve.

Makes approximately 8 cups

RICH PLUM CAKE ♪♪♪

Digory describes the Wood between the Worlds as being "as rich as plum cake." How are you going to understand this figure of speech if you've never had plum cake? (*The Magician's Nephew*, chapter 3).

Plum used to refer to any dried fruit, but especially raisins, and that usage still survives today in England in the names of such foods as plum cakes and plum puddings. Plum cakes are supposed to taste better after they have aged for a few months, but this version is also delicious fresh out of the oven. Fruitcakes can be stored for a very long time, and Queen Victoria was known to wait a year before tasting a fruitcake she had been given as a gift to demonstrate her self-control. Well, she certainly had more self-control than I do—I can't even wait for it to finish cooling.

2½ cups all-purpose flour

½ cup ground almonds

½ teaspoon salt

¾ teaspoons baking powder

1½ teaspoons ground cinnamon

½ teaspoon ground nutmeg

¼ teaspoon ground cloves

¼ teaspoon ground allspice

16 tablespoons (1 cup) butter, at
   room temperature

1½ cups sugar

3 large eggs, at room temperature

½ cup orange marmalade

¼ cup brandy, plus an additional ¼
   cup brandy for storing, if desired

⅓ cup raisins

⅓ cup golden raisins

⅓ cup dried currants (see sidebar) or
   dried sweetened cranberries

⅓ cup chopped walnuts

1. Preheat the oven to 300°F. Grease a 9-inch springform pan and line the bottom and sides with parchment paper. Greasing the bottom and sides first helps the paper stick to the pan.

For years, I thought currants referred to red or black currants, which are for the most part unavailable here in the United States. It turns out that they are really tiny raisins, like the Zante currants you can find next to the raisins in the dried fruit section of the grocery store. Not knowing any better, I used dried sweetened cranberries in many recipes that traditionally use currants. However, I like this substitution so much that I'm recommending it here if you can't find the Zante currants.

2. Whisk together the flour, ground almonds, salt, baking powder, and spices. In a separate mixing bowl, using an electric mixer, beat the butter and sugar until light and fluffy, scraping down the sides as needed, about 5 minutes. Add the eggs one at a time, beating after each until incorporated and scraping down the sides as needed. Add a third of the flour mixture and mix on the slowest speed until combined. Then add the marmalade, half of the remaining flour mixture, the brandy, and the rest of the remaining flour mixture, mixing on the slowest speed after each addition just until combined. Stir in the chopped fruit and nuts. Give a final stir with a rubber spatula.

3. Scrape the mixture into the prepared pan and smooth to the edges of the pan with a rubber spatula. Bake for 2½ hours, until the cake feels set when pressed lightly or a cake tester comes out clean.

4. Allow the cake to cool completely before removing it from the pan. To remove the cake, unlatch the side and lift off. Run a sharp knife along the bottom. Invert the cake onto a sheet of aluminum foil and lift off the bottom of the pan. Peel off the parchment. Wrap in aluminum foil and then seal in a plastic bag.

5. The cake will keep, tightly sealed, at room temperature for 2 weeks. To store the cake for up to a year, turn the cake upside down and poke holes into the cake with a skewer. Pour ¼ cup brandy over the cake and rewrap as previously directed. Store the cake upside down. Repeat this treatment once a month until ready to use.

Makes 1 9-inch cake

TEA WITH TUMNUS

· Tender Soft–Boiled Eggs · Sardines on Toast ·
· Buttered Toast and Toast with Honey ·Sugar–Dusted Sponge Tea Cake ·

In playing a game of hide and seek, Lucy has stumbled into the magical world of Narnia. No one will believe her, of course, but for the moment, she enjoys a delightful tea with Tumnus the Faun, unaware of his evil intent (*The Lion, the Witch and the Wardrobe*, chapter 2).

TENDER SOFT-BOILED EGGS

Lucy had a soft-boiled brown egg. There is no difference between white and brown eggs except for the breed of hens that lay them, so you can use white or brown.

1. To soft-boil large eggs, remove them from the refrigerator 30 minutes before cooking to bring them to room temperature.

2. Bring water to boil in a pot. While the water is heating, fill a large bowl with cold water. When the water is boiling, carefully lower the eggs into the pot in a single layer.

3. Boil gently for 4 minutes; then remove the eggs with a slotted spoon and dip them into the cold water for 30 seconds.

SARDINES ON TOAST, BUTTERED TOAST, AND TOAST WITH HONEY

When you serve the tea, make sure to include platters of buttered toast and toast with honey, as well as sardines to eat them with.

SUGAR-DUSTED SPONGE TEA CAKE *♪♪♪*

6 large eggs, separated, at room
   temperature
¼ teaspoon salt
¼ teaspoon cream of tartar
1 teaspoon pure vanilla extract

¾ cup sugar, divided
Grated zest and juice of 1 lemon
⅔ cup vegetable oil
1¼ cup cake flour, sifted

1. Preheat the oven to 350°F. For this recipe, use a 10-inch tube pan, light metal (as opposed to dark), and *not* nonstick.

2. Beat the egg whites on medium-high speed with the salt, cream of tartar, and vanilla until soft mounds begin to form. Gradually add ½ cup of the sugar and continue to beat on medium-high speed until stiff peaks form. Be careful not to overbeat the egg whites (the egg whites should be glossy; if they turn dry and cottony, they're overbeaten and you'll have to start over). Set aside.

3. In a separate mixing bowl, beat the egg yolks, remaining sugar, and lemon zest and juice on medium-high speed until thick and lemon-colored, about 10 minutes. Slowly pour in the oil; the mixture will thicken and lighten further. Adding the oil takes a good few minutes, because you need to let the oil thoroughly mix in between dribbles. Scrape down the sides as needed. Add the sifted flour in 2 batches, stirring on the slowest speed to combine. Finish mixing by folding with a rubber spatula.

4. Add a quarter of the beaten egg whites to the yolk mixture to lighten it and whisk until combined. Gently fold in the remaining egg whites with a rubber spatula. Scrape the mixture into the pan. Tap the pan lightly on the counter to eliminate air bubbles.

5. Bake for 45 minutes or until light golden brown. Remove from the oven and immediately invert over a wine bottle or similar stand. Leave the cake over the wine bottle until completely cooled.

6. To remove the cake from the pan, run a knife along the outer and inner edges.

Makes 1 10-inch cake, which will feed 10 dainty eaters or 5 hearty ones (or just 1 or 2 serious cake lovers)

SNACK WITH THE WHITE WITCH

· *Sweet and Creamy Hot Vanilla* · *Turkish Delight* ·

The White Witch raises her wand, about to turn Edmund into stone, no doubt, when she suddenly has a change of heart. Edmund may prove very useful. So she puts on a motherly type of concern and invites him onto her sleigh to have a hot drink, some Turkish delight, and a chat (*The Lion, the Witch and the Wardrobe*, chapter 4).

·•⦂[sweet and creamy hot vanilla ⸙⸙⸙]⦂•·

You may be looking at this recipe and thinking, "Sweet and creamy hot vanilla *what?*" But if we have hot chocolate, why not hot vanilla? I imagine that this is exactly what the creamy hot drink the White Witch gave Edmund tasted like.

2 cups whole milk	*1 tablespoon cornstarch*
¼ cup sugar	*½ teaspoon pure vanilla extract*
¼ cup heavy cream	*Grated nutmeg, optional, for serving*

1. Combine the milk and sugar in a small or medium saucepan and bring to a simmer. In a small mixing bowl, whisk together the heavy cream and cornstarch until smooth. Add the cream mixture to the milk mixture, stirring constantly over medium-high heat, until thickened and bubbling, 5 to 10 minutes. Remove from the heat and stir in the vanilla extract.

2. Divide the hot drink among 3 to 4 teacups. Sprinkle the grated nutmeg on top, if using. Serve immediately.

Serves 3 to 4

·❧ Turkish Delight 🥄🥄🥄 ❧·

The White Witch enchants the Turkish delight she gives to Edmund so that he will sell his whole family to her for more. But this confection is so good, she probably didn't even need to enchant it. As its name indicates, Turkish delight comes from Turkey, where it's called *lokum*. The chief confectioner to the sultan possibly invented it in the late 1700s, and it spread to Europe and quickly became popular there. Fortunately, you don't have to sell your family to get some—you can make it yourself!

Sugar Syrup
4 cups sugar
1 teaspoon cream of tartar
1 cup water

Flavoring
4 teaspoons rose water or
    orange
blossom water

Cornstarch Paste
1 cup cornstarch
Juice of 1 lemon
3 cups water

Coating
1 cup confectioners' sugar
½ cup cornstarch

1. Grease a 9-inch-by-13-inch pan and line it with plastic wrap. Greasing the bottom and sides helps the plastic stick to the pan. Set aside until needed.

2. To make the sugar syrup, combine the sugar, cream of tartar, and water in a large saucepan. Cook over high heat, stirring constantly, until the sugar is dissolved, 5 to 10 minutes. Wash the sides of the pan with a pastry brush dipped in hot water and clip a candy thermometer to the side of the pan. Continue cooking over medium-high heat without stirring until the mixture reaches 290°F. Remove from the heat and stir until the temperature drops a few degrees to prevent scorching. The temperature will first rise a few more degrees and then fall. Cover the saucepan.

3. To make the cornstarch paste, whisk together the cornstarch, lemon juice, and water in a large saucepan. Cook over medium heat, whisking constantly, until the mixture turns into a thick paste, 5 to 10 minutes. Pour the sugar syrup into the cornstarch paste in 5 or 6 batches, whisking after each batch until smooth. Raise the temperature to medium-high and continue cooking, stirring constantly with a wooden spoon to prevent scorching, until the mixture turns a light golden color and is very thick and gelatinous, about 30 minutes.

4. Remove the pan from the heat, add the rose water or orange blossom water, and stir until smooth.

5. Scrape the mixture into the prepared pan and spread with the wooden spoon. The mixture will be hard to spread, so don't worry if it's imperfect. Cover with plastic wrap and cool completely at room temperature, 5 hours or overnight.

6. When the candy is completely cool, remove the slab from the pan and cut into 1-inch pieces (make 7 cuts along the width and 11 cuts along the length). Sift together the confectioners' sugar and cornstarch in a large mixing bowl and whisk to combine. Toss several pieces of the candy at a time into the confectioners' sugar–cornstarch mixture to coat. Store in an airtight container between layers of plastic wrap or parchment paper.

Makes 96 pieces

On the Run
with the Beavers

· Boiled Ham with Apricot Sauce · Packet of Tea and Sugar
· Hearty Wheat Bread ·

As soon as the Beavers and Pevensies realize Edmund has betrayed them, Mr. Beaver announces they must flee, as the White Witch will lose no time setting out to track them down. Mrs. Beaver quickly gathers provisions for their journey to meet Aslan (*The Lion, the Witch and the Wardrobe*, chapter 10).

·≍] Boiled Ham with Apricot Sauce ♪ ♪ ♪ [≍·

THANKS TO CHEF CHRIS KOCH FOR THIS RECIPE.

1 (12- to 14-pound) smoked country ham (such as Smithfield)
2 (15-ounce) cans apricots in heavy syrup

1 teaspoon ground cloves
½ teaspoon ground allspice
1 teaspoon ground cinnamon

1. To boil, place the ham in a large pot or Dutch oven in which the meat will fit fairly tightly, and then cover it with cold water. Slowly bring the liquid to a boil, skimming the foam that forms on top. Drain the ham, return the ham to the pot, refill with water, and bring back to a boil.

2. As soon as the ham reaches the second boil, reduce the heat to low so that the liquid is gently simmering. Cover and let simmer for 20 to 25 minutes per pound (4 to 5 hours). Add water as necessary to keep the ham covered with liquid.

3. Cook until the ham reaches an internal temperature of 155°F or when it can be easily pierced with a knife and the meat starts to separate from the bones. Transfer to a large platter or cutting board and cover with foil.

4. In a medium saucepan, combine the apricots with syrup and spices. Bring to a boil, then reduce the heat and simmer for 10 minutes. Transfer to a blender (in batches, if necessary) and puree until smooth.

5. Slice the ham and serve with the sauce.

Serves 24

·⊰[PACKET OF TEA AND SUGAR]⊱·

When you serve the ham and bread, don't forget the tea! Mrs. Beaver made sure to include a packet of tea leaves and some sugar to take along on the escape journey from the White Witch.

·⊰[HEARTY WHEAT BREAD 🥄🥄🥄]⊱·

Bread, like eggs, is such a staple in diets both ancient and modern that it has taken an important place in both religion and superstition. Before eating bread, Orthodox Jews engage in a ritual of hand washing and blessings. In parts of Western Europe, hanging a loaf in your home on Good Friday was supposed to protect you from evil spirits, and the famous hot cross buns have a cross cut into them for the same reason. Since baking bread in Anglo-Saxon culture was a woman's job, the Anglo-Saxon word for women means "loaf kneaders" (*hlaefdige*). Mrs. Beaver serves this staff of life to the Pevensies for dinner and also packs along some bread for their journey (*The Lion, the Witch and the Wardrobe*, chapters 7 and 10).

1 tablespoon or 1 packet yeast
¼ cup plus 1 teaspoon sugar, divided
¼ cup warm water
1¾ cups all-purpose flour
1 cup whole-wheat flour
1 teaspoon salt

½ cup whole milk, at room temperature
4 tablespoons (¼ cup) butter, at room temperature
1 egg, at room temperature

1. Combine the yeast, I teaspoon sugar, and warm water in a small bowl and set aside until puffy.

2. Whisk together the all-purpose flour and whole-wheat flour, ¼ cup sugar, and salt in the mixing bowl of a stand mixer. Fit the mixer with the dough hook. Add the milk, butter, egg, and yeast mixture. Knead until smooth and the dough cleans the sides of the bowl, about 10 minutes. The dough can also be kneaded by hand.

3. Remove the dough from the bowl and knead by hand for a few seconds. Place in an oiled bowl, turning to coat the dough. Cover with plastic wrap and keep in a warm, draft-free place until doubled in size, 1½ to 2 hours.

4. Spray a medium loaf pan with baking spray with flour. Turn out the dough onto a lightly floured work surface. Form it into a loaf and place it in the loaf pan. Set aside until doubled in size, 1½ to 2 hours.

5. Preheat the oven to 350°F. Bake for 25 to 35 minutes, until light golden brown. Remove to a wire rack to cool. This bread is best eaten the day it is made.

Makes 1 loaf

CHRISTMAS TEA FROM FATHER CHRISTMAS

· Best–Ever Ham Sandwiches · Tea with Cream and Sugar Cubes ·

When the White Witch reigns, it is always winter but never Christmas. Aslan's influence begins to be felt when the Beavers and Pevensies bump into Father Christmas, who leaves them with gifts and a delightful tea (*The Lion, the Witch and the Wardrobe*, chapter 10).

BEST-EVER HAM SANDWICHES

Be sure to use the ham and bread recipes listed previously (from the menu "On the Run with the Beavers" on pages 49 and 50) to make the sandwiches.

*8 slices bread, from the Hearty
    Wheat Bread recipe, or good-
    quality sandwich bread*
*4 to 8 thin slices ham, from the Boiled
    Ham with Apricot Sauce recipe*

*¼ cup apricot sauce, from the Boiled
    Ham with Apricot Sauce recipe*
English mustard
4 large lettuce leaves

1. For each sandwich, spread one slice of bread with 1 tablespoon apricot sauce and the other with the mustard. Top one slice with a lettuce leaf, then 1 or 2 slices of ham, then the other slice of bread. Slice in half diagonally to form triangles.
2. Repeat with the remaining ingredients.

Serves 4

TEA WITH CREAM AND SUGAR CUBES

Make sure to have a teapot filled with piping hot tea, a bowl of sugar cubes, and a pitcher of cream to go with the ham sandwiches in this hearty tea.

High Tea after Battle

· Hearty Meaty Pea Soup · Shepherd's Pie · Cornish Pasties ·
· Jam Roly Poly with Custard · Cinnamon-Raisin Scones · Tea ·

The battle is over; the witch is dead. Tired and hungry, the battle-worn children sit down to a high tea that Aslan mysteriously provides (*The Lion, the Witch and the Wardrobe*, chapter 17). The foods here represent a typical high tea, which is tea and dinner combined. Don't forget the tea as you're preparing this meal!

·❧[Hearty Meaty Pea Soup 🥄🥄🥄]❧·

Language evolves, and what one generation considers a mistake may be perfectly acceptable to a later generation. Thus it is with the word *pea*. The original singular Old English word was *pease*, but because it sounds plural, the singular became *pea*. Never mind. A rose by any other name—I mean, a pea soup by any other name will taste just as good.

1½ pounds chuck steak, cut into ½-inch cubes, or beef stewing cubes
2 tablespoons vegetable oil
1 onion, chopped
1 (1-pound) bag dried split peas, rinsed
½ cup pearled barley, rinsed
3 cloves garlic, minced
1 medium carrot, chopped
1½ teaspoons salt
¼ teaspoon freshly ground black pepper
¼ teaspoon dried thyme
2 quarts chicken broth

1. Spray a Dutch oven or large pot with cooking spray and sear the meat over high heat until crusty brown on all sides, about 3 minutes per side. Transfer the meat to a large plate and reduce the heat to medium.

2. Add the oil to the skillet. Add the chopped onion and cook, stirring frequently, until browned, about 10 minutes.

3. Add the meat back to the pot along with the peas, barley, garlic, carrot, salt,

pepper, thyme, and chicken broth. Bring to a boil, then reduce the heat to low and simmer for 2½ hours, stirring occasionally to prevent scorching.

4. Serve with thick slices of crusty bread, if desired.

Serves 8

···❧[SHEPHERD'S PIE ♪♪♪]ೋ···

It's not hard to guess how this dish got its name. If you're a shepherd hanging out with sheep all day, you may occasionally be tempted to eat some of them, and what better way than to bake them into a pie? Technically, a similar pie made with beef is called cottage pie, but today most people call both types shepherd's pie.

TOPPING

4 large baking potatoes, peeled and
   cut into quarters
4 eggs
½ cup vegetable oil

¼ cup chicken broth
2 teaspoons salt
¼ teaspoon freshly ground black
   pepper

FILLING

1 pound ground lamb or beef
3 tablespoons vegetable oil
1 onion, chopped
2 celery ribs, chopped
½ large green pepper or 1 small green
   pepper, chopped
10 ounces mushrooms, sliced

1 medium carrot, chopped
4 garlic cloves, minced
2 cups chicken broth
¼ cup tomato paste
1 teaspoon salt
¼ teaspoon freshly ground black
   pepper

1. To make the topping, place the potatoes into a large saucepan and fill with water to cover. Bring to a boil, reduce the heat to medium, and simmer, covered, until the potatoes are soft and easily pierced with a fork, about 25 minutes. Drain the potatoes and mash.

2. In a separate bowl, whisk together the eggs, oil, broth, salt, and pepper. Pour into the hot potatoes and mix well. Set aside.

3. Adjust the oven rack to the middle position and place a baking sheet on the rack to catch drips. Preheat the oven to 350°F.

4. To make the filling, heat a large skillet over medium-high heat and brown the lamb or beef, pushing down with a wooden spoon or potato masher until browned and crumbly, about 10 minutes. Transfer to a mixing bowl and set aside. Add the oil to the skillet and heat over high heat. Add the onion, celery, green pepper, mushrooms, and carrot and cook, stirring frequently, until the water cooks out and the mixture browns, about 15 minutes. Add the garlic and cook another few seconds, until fragrant. Add the broth, tomato paste, salt, and pepper and cook, stirring constantly, until smooth, about 5 minutes. Remove from the heat and stir in the meat.

5. Pour the meat mixture into a deep 10-inch round baking dish and spread evenly. Spread the potato mixture on top. Place the pie on the baking sheet in the oven and bake for 1 hour, until the crust is golden brown and the juices are bubbling. Let the pie rest for 15 minutes before serving.

Serves 8

·⊰[CORNISH PASTIES 🥄🥄🥄]⊱·

According to radio personality Michelle McKormick, English immigrants introduced this type of meat pasty to Michigan. Pasties were popular in England too, especially in Cornwall, where women would prepare these for their husbands, as the pasties were easy to take along to the mines where they worked. A Cornish housewife would stamp her husband's initials on his pasty so he could identify his own in the large communal oven, where the pasties were kept warm until lunch break.

3 tablespoons vegetable oil
8 ounces chuck steak, finely chopped
  (not ground)
1 onion, chopped

5 ounces mushrooms, sliced
1 medium carrot, chopped
2 to 3 green cabbage leaves, chopped
  (or 1 cup shredded)

1 large red-skin potato, peeled and
   chopped
½ teaspoon salt
¼ teaspoon freshly ground black pepper
2 cloves garlic, minced

¼ teaspoon dried thyme
1 tablespoon chopped fresh dill
1 (1-pound) package frozen puff
   pastry dough, thawed and cut
   into 5-inch squares

1. Heat the oil in a large skillet. Add the chopped meat, vegetables, salt, and pepper and cook over high heat, stirring frequently, until the juice is cooked out and the mixture browns, about 20 minutes. Add the garlic and stir until fragrant, a few seconds. Remove from the heat and stir in the thyme and dill. Cool to room temperature.

2. Preheat the oven to 425°F and line a baking sheet with parchment paper. Fill the pastry squares with 2 tablespoons of the filling. Wet the edges, fold over to form triangles, and press with your fingers or a fork to seal. Cut slits to form vents. Bake for 20 to 25 minutes, rotating the baking sheet halfway through baking, until golden brown.

Makes 10 pasties

·∘][Jam ROLY POLY WITH Custard][∘·

A roly poly pudding is a suet pudding (don't worry; this recipe uses butter instead) in which the dough is rolled out, a filling is spread over it, it's rolled up, and then it's steamed. I tried to steam it in a cloth, but couldn't figure out how to keep the water out. Fortunately, today's roly poly puddings are usually baked, so you can bake this one and still feel respectable. (And it's better baked anyway; it would lose its flakiness with steaming.)

Roly Poly Pudding 🥄🥄🥄

2 cups all-purpose flour
¼ cup sugar
½ teaspoon salt
12 tablespoons (¾ cup) butter,
   chilled and cut into chunks

⅓ cup ice water
1 cup raspberry jam
1 egg, beaten with 1 tablespoon
   water

Warm Custard Sauce 🥄🥄🥄

2 cups whole milk

⅓ cup sugar

4 egg yolks

1 tablespoon cornstarch

1½ teaspoons pure vanilla extract

1 tablespoon butter

1. To make the dough, place the flour, sugar, and salt in the bowl of a food processor. Pulse to combine. Scatter the chunks of butter over the flour mixture and pulse until the mixture resembles a coarse meal, like wet sand, but with some larger clumps of butter remaining. Turn the mixture into a large mixing bowl. Sprinkle the ice water on top and fold with a spatula until the mixture starts to clump. Form into a disk and wrap in plastic wrap. Chill in the refrigerator at least 2 hours or up to 3 days.

2. Preheat the oven to 425°F and line a baking sheet with parchment paper. Roll out the dough on a generously floured work surface (make sure to flour the top of the dough as well) to an ⅛-inch-thick rectangle. Spread the jam to within an inch of the borders. Roll the long side up, dab water along the edge, and press to seal. Seal the ends and tuck under. Brush the beaten egg over the top and transfer to the prepared baking sheet.

3. Bake for 10 minutes. Reduce the temperature to 350°F and bake another 40 minutes, until golden brown.

4. While the roly poly is baking, make the custard sauce. Heat the milk and sugar in a medium saucepan over medium heat, stirring until dissolved, about 5 minutes. Continue cooking until steaming hot but not bubbling. Whisk together the yolks and cornstarch until smooth. Pour 1 cup of the hot milk mixture into the yolk mixture while whisking constantly, then pour the yolk mixture into the saucepan, stirring constantly. Cook over medium heat, stirring constantly, until the mixture is thick and bubbling, another 5 minutes. Remove from the heat and stir in the vanilla extract and butter. Pour through a sieve to ensure a perfectly smooth custard.

5. Serve the roly poly with warm custard sauce.

Serves 8

⋅⋅≈] CINNamon-RaISIn Scones ♪♪♪ [≈⋅⋅

Pronounced "scon" in Scotland (and originating there as well), scones today are popular with tea in England. This recipe is a sweeter, richer version of the classic teatime scone.

2 cups flour
⅓ cup sugar
½ teaspoon salt
1 teaspoon ground cinnamon

16 tablespoons (1 cup) butter, chilled
    and cut into chunks
⅓ cup heavy cream
1 cup raisins

1. Adjust the oven rack to the middle position and preheat the oven to 425°F. Line a baking sheet with parchment paper. Place the flour, sugar, salt, and cinnamon into the bowl of a food processor and pulse a few times to combine. Scatter the butter on top and pulse about 10 times, until the mixture resembles a coarse yellow meal like crumbs with some larger clumps of butter remaining.

2. Turn the mixture out into a mixing bowl. Add the heavy cream and fold with a rubber spatula until the dough starts clumping together. Fold in the raisins. Turn the dough out onto a floured work surface and pat into a rectangle that is about 13 inches by 4½ inches. Cut the dough into 12 triangular wedges and transfer them to the prepared baking sheet.

3. Bake for 10 minutes, rotating the baking sheet halfway through the baking time. Reduce the temperature to 350°F and bake another 20 minutes, rotating again halfway through the baking time, until light golden. Cool on a wire rack.

Makes 1 dozen

WHEN SHASTA IS MISTAKEN FOR CORIN

· Iced Sherbet (Creamy Orange Sherbet) ·

Shasta and his talking horse, Bree, have joined up with Aravis and her talking horse, Hwin. When they arrive in the great city of Tashbaan, Shasta is separated from the rest by the crowd, where the visiting Narnian royal family immediately mistakes him for Prince Corin. This turns out not to be so bad after all, when he is fussed over and given iced sherbet (*The Horse and His Boy*, chapter 4).

ICED SHERBET (CREAMY ORANGE SHERBET)

With their curved swords and dark skin, the Calormenes appear to be Arabians. And iced sherbet certainly fits in with the climate in Arabia, especially considering that Arabs invented this delicious iced dessert or drink. In fact, people served sherbet, or sorbet—both of which come from the Arabic word *sharbât*—in fancy cups to mark special occasions. Today, people argue about whether sherbet and sorbet are one and the same, with some arguing that sherbet must contain milk or cream and sorbet must not, and others arguing that no matter what you call it, no dairy ingredients may be added. I like the idea of adding dairy to sherbet, so you get the benefit of this creamier yet still icy version. You will need an ice cream maker for this recipe.

1 cup heavy cream
⅓ cup confectioners' sugar
1 teaspoon orange extract

1 teaspoon pure vanilla extract
2 cups freshly squeezed orange juice
    (from about 8 oranges)

I. Whip the cream with the sugar and extracts until soft peaks form. Continue whipping while slowly pouring in the juice against the side of the bowl, scraping down the sides as needed.

2. Pour into an ice cream maker and freeze according to the manufacturer's instructions. Scrape into an airtight container and freeze until firm.

Makes about 1 quart

ARAVIS AND LASARALEEN HAVE A SNACK

· Apple Jelly and Whipped Cream · Scrumptious Strawberry Ice ·

After Aravis and Shasta become separated, Aravis is recognized by her old friend Lasaraleen. Aravis is frantic for her help, but Lasaraleen is so silly that Aravis is almost ready to tear her hair out. Instead of listening to her story, Lasaraleen insists on a long bath and a meal consisting "chiefly of the whipped cream and jelly and fruit and ice sort" (*The Horse and His Boy*, chapter 7).

··≺] APPLE JELLY WITH WHIPPED cream ♩♩♩ [≻··

Dessert jellies, unlike the jelly you use in your peanut butter and jelly sandwich, are descendants from a medieval dish called calf's foot jelly, which is a broth set with gelatin. In the nineteenth century, it was popular to serve different colored jellies laid in strips in one dish. Today, fruit juice set with gelatin and served with whipped cream makes for a quick and simple dessert.

2 cups apple juice, divided
1 tablespoon (1 packet) powdered
*   gelatin*
½ cup apple juice concentrate

½ cup heavy cream
2 tablespoons confectioners' sugar
½ teaspoon pure vanilla extract

1. Pour ½ cup of the apple juice into a bowl and sprinkle the gelatin on top. Set aside to soften, about 5 minutes.

2. Pour the remaining apple juice and apple juice concentrate into a small saucepan and cook over medium-high heat until hot. Add the softened gelatin mixture and whisk until completely dissolved.

3. Divide the mixture among 4 teacups and chill until firm, about 4 hours or overnight.

4. Before serving, whip the cream, confectioners' sugar, and vanilla until soft peaks form. Divide the whipped cream among the 4 teacups.

Serves 4

⋅⋗⟧ SCRUMPTIOUS STRAWBERRY ICE 🥄🥄🥄 ⟦⋖⋅

1 pound strawberries, fresh or
frozen, crowns removed if fresh
and thawed if frozen

½ cup sugar
½ cup water
Juice of 1 lemon

1. Place the strawberries, sugar, water, and lemon juice in a blender or food processor and process until smooth. Pour the mixture into a sieve and push through the sieve with a spatula, pressing down on the mixture to extract as much juice as possible. Discard the seeds and pulp. You should have about 2 cups of the strawberry mixture.

2. Carefully pour the mixture into ice cube trays. It's easier to avoid spills if you first pour the mixture into a large measuring cup or a bowl with a spout. The mixture should fill up about 1½ ice cube trays. Freeze until firm, 4 to 5 hours or overnight.

3. Before serving, remove the trays from the freezer. To release the ice cubes, hold the tray upside down under a stream of hot water for a few seconds, then bang it over a large plate. Crush the ice cubes in a blender, using 4 cubes per serving. Serve immediately.

Serves 5

FOOD FOR FLIGHT WITH PRINCE CASPIAN

· Mediterranean Cold Sliced Chicken · Cold Roast Venison ·
· Homemade Sandwich Bread · Apples and Wine (Ginger Beer for Kids)·

Doctor Cornelius wakes Prince Caspian in the dead of night to tell him he must flee, now that his usurping uncle King Miraz has had a son whom he will wish to see on the throne. Caspian's tutor puts together a bundle of food and money for him to take on his flight to Archenland to seek the aid of its king (*Prince Caspian*, chapter 5).

⌐ MEDITERRANEAN COLD SLICED CHICKEN ⌐

Mrs. Beeton's Book of Household Management, a nineteenth-century cook-book, has a whole section on cold meat cookery, but that refers mostly to cooking with leftover meats. The chicken that Prince Caspian takes along with him, left from that night's dinner, has grown cold, but chicken can be quite good eaten cold, if done right. This recipe, inspired by the race, dress, and customs of the Telmarines, reflects Mediterranean flavors.

3 tablespoons vegetable oil

1 onion, sliced

2 garlic cloves, minced

1 tablespoon all-purpose flour

1 cup chicken broth

½ teaspoon ground cumin, plus more
   for sprinkling

½ teaspoon ground coriander

¼ teaspoon ground ginger

¼ teaspoon salt, plus more for
   sprinkling

¼ teaspoon freshly ground black
   pepper, plus more for sprinkling

1 lemon, thinly sliced

2 pieces bone-in, skin-on split chicken
   breast

1 tablespoon olive oil

Garlic powder, for sprinkling on chicken

1. Preheat the oven to 450°F. Heat the oil in a large skillet. Add the onion and cook over high heat, stirring frequently, until browned, about 10 minutes. Add the garlic and cook, stirring constantly, until fragrant, a few seconds. Add the flour and stir to combine. Pour in the chicken broth, stirring constantly. Add ½ teaspoon cumin, the coriander, the ginger, ¼ teaspoon salt, and ¼ teaspoon pepper. Cook over medium-high heat, stirring frequently, until thickened, about 7 minutes. Pour into a small baking dish and layer the lemon slices over the sauce.

2. Rub the chicken breasts with the olive oil and lightly sprinkle with the salt, pepper, garlic powder, and cumin. Place the chicken on top of the lemon slices. Bake for 30 to 35 minutes, until a meat thermometer inserted into thickest part of the breast registers 160°F.

3. Cool to room temperature. Transfer the chicken breasts to a cutting board. Remove the meat from the bone and cut into ½-inch-thick slices. Place the slices back into the sauce to pick up some of the flavor. Serve at room temperature or cold. If desired, serve the chicken warm and pass the sauce at the table separately.

Serves 2 to 4

·⊰[COLD ROAST VENISON]⊱·

THANKS TO CHEF CHRIS KOCH FOR THIS RECIPE.

According to the World's Healthiest Foods website (www.whfoods.com), just 4 ounces of venison provides over 80 percent of your daily protein needs for about 200 calories, and with very little fat (only 2.2 grams of saturated fat). It also provides about a third of your daily iron. It's a rich food source, which may be why people have been hunting deer for venison since the Stone Age.

½ cup sherry, red wine, or cider vinegar
2 cloves garlic, minced
1 tablespoon salt

½ cup red wine
2 tablespoons light or dark brown sugar
1 teaspoon mustard (any kind)

1 tablespoon Worcestershire sauce
¼ cup white vinegar or lemon juice
1 large onion, sliced

4 pounds leg of venison, boned,
*   rolled, and tied*

1. Mix all the ingredients except for the venison together in a large bowl or large pot. Add the venison and enough water for the marinade to just cover the venison. Turn the venison to coat with the marinade. Using a fork, poke holes all over the surface of the venison. The deeper the holes, the deeper the marinade will penetrate. Add enough cold water to cover the venison. Cover with plastic wrap and refrigerate for 8 hours or overnight.

2. Remove the venison from the marinade and discard the liquid.

3. To cook on a gas rotisserie, preheat to 350°F. Place the roast on the spit and cook for 1 hour or to the desired degree of doneness (internal temperature of 140°F for medium rare, 150°F for medium, or 165°F for well done).

4. To cook in the oven, preheat the oven to 450°F. Heat an ovenproof skillet over high heat. Brown the venison on all sides, about 4 minutes per side. Transfer the skillet to the oven. Roast for 45 minutes or to the desired degree of doneness.

5. Remove the roast from the spit or oven and let it rest for 20 minutes (to let the juices redistribute). Slice the roast and place on a serving platter or in a storage container. Cover and refrigerate. Serve chilled with a sweet preserve or sauce such as cherry, plum, or apricot, or with your favorite accompaniment.

Serves 6 to 8

·⋅[HOMEMADE SANDWICH BREAD *↑↑↑*]⋅·

Wheat flour, because of its high gluten content, is best suited for bread baking. While wheat flour has been used in bread baking throughout history, bread was also made from spelt, rye, and barley. The Romans figured out a way to harness waterpower to mill their flour, but it was a tedious task—especially to sieve the flour—until the 1800s, when steel rollers were invented. Until then, white flour was extremely difficult to come by. But that would certainly not have been a problem in King Miraz's court.

4 tablespoons (¼ cup) butter
1 cup whole milk
3 cups all-purpose flour

1 tablespoon (1 packet) instant yeast
1 teaspoon salt

1. Heat the butter and milk in a small saucepan until the butter melts. Keep warm, but don't use when hot, or the heat will kill the yeast.

2. Whisk together the flour, yeast, and salt in a large mixing bowl. Add the milk mixture and knead in a stand mixer fitted with the dough hook or by hand for 10 minutes, until smooth and elastic.

3. Place the dough in an oiled bowl, turning to coat the dough. Cover with plastic wrap and leave in a warm, draft-free place until doubled in size, 1½ to 2 hours.

4. Spray a loaf pan with baking spray and set aside. Turn the dough out onto a lightly floured work surface, shape into a loaf, and place into the prepared loaf pan. Leave to rise until doubled in size, 1½ to 2 hours.

5. Adjust the oven rack to the middle position and preheat the oven to 350°F. Bake the bread for 30 minutes, rotating the pan halfway through baking, until the bread is a pale golden color. Invert onto a wire rack to cool.

Makes 1 loaf

·⟩[APPLES AND GINGER BEER]⟨·

Be sure to take along apples and some sort of beverage when you go out into the wide world to seek your fortune. Try the ginger beer recipe (from the "The Sweets They Had in Those Days" menu on page 41). Grown-ups can bring wine.

DRINK FROM TRUFFLEHUNTER THE BADGER

· Frothy Hot Chocolate ·

After nearly being killed by a storm in the forest, Caspian awakes to hear voices debating whether to finish him off or not. One of the voices decides to give him something to drink. After this vague figure lifts up Caspian's head to help him drink something sweet and hot, Caspian gets a shock when its face comes into focus: it's a badger, not a human! And it talks! (*Prince Caspian*, chapter 5).

··ᴐ⟦ FROTHY HOT CHOCOLATE ♪♪♪ ⟧ɔ··

Something hot and sweet could be lots of things, but to me, a confirmed chocoholic, the most comforting drink in the world is hot chocolate. The Mayans used to put ground chili peppers in their hot chocolate (yes, the drink has been around that long), and only the nobility were allowed to drink it. To make it frothy, they would pour it into a drinking vessel from a great height (who doesn't love the froth on top?). The Aztecs added honey to sweeten their hot chocolate. The Spanish explorers brought chocolate back with them to Europe, where its popularity quickly spread.

½ cup heavy cream

2 ounces bittersweet chocolate, chopped

2 tablespoons cocoa powder, Dutch processed preferred, plus more for dusting if desired

⅓ cup sugar

¼ teaspoon salt

2 cups water

2 cups whole milk

1 teaspoon pure vanilla extract

4 tablespoons whipped cream, optional, for serving

I. Heat the cream in a small saucepan until it bubbles around the edges. Place the chocolate in a mixing bowl. Pour the cream over the chocolate and let it stand a few minutes; then whisk until smooth.

Variations

Rum Mocha: Add 1 tablespoon instant coffee, regular or decaf, with the cocoa powder when combining the cocoa powder, sugar, and salt. Proceed as directed, but omit the vanilla and add ½ teaspoon rum extract in its place.

Cinnamon: Use a cinnamon stick as a stirrer.

Ultrasmooth: Replace the bittersweet chocolate with white chocolate when creating the ganache.

2. In a medium saucepan, combine 2 tablespoons cocoa powder, the sugar, and the salt. Stir in the water and cook over medium-high heat until hot and beginning to boil. Add the milk and cook just until hot. Remove from the heat and whisk in the ganache (the chocolate and heavy cream mixture). Add the vanilla and whisk to combine.

3. Whisk until frothy and pour into mugs. Top with a tablespoon of whipped cream and a dusting of cocoa powder, if desired.

Serves 4

SNACK ON THE SHIP IN THE PICTURE

· Hot Spiced Wine or Mulled Cider ·

· Plumptree's Vitaminized Nerve Food (Health Bars) · Wholemeal Sugar Biscuits ·

Edmund and Lucy are warming up with hot spiced wine after falling through the picture into the sea (grown-ups allowed kids to drink wine in those days), but Eustace is miserable and wailing for his Plumptree's Vitaminized Nerve Food. Miserably sea-sick, he spends his time moaning in his cabin among the casks of apples, wine, cheese, nuts, and biscuits (*The Voyage of the Dawn Treader*, chapters 1 and 2).

HOT SPICED WINE (FOR GROWN-UPS)

You can find a recipe for hot spiced wine (*ypocras*) in a 1390s cookbook called *The Forme of Cury* and in the famous *Mrs. Beeton's Book of Household Management*. The Roman cookbook writer Apicius also offers an unusual but fascinating recipe that includes saffron and laurel leaves and crushed roasted date stones and was filtered through charcoal, so we know people have enjoyed this type of drink for a long time. Very popular in Europe for Christmas, hot spiced wine is a wonderfully warming winter drink.

2 cups dry red wine
2 tablespoons honey
1 cinnamon stick

6 whole cloves
8 allspice berries

1. Combine all ingredients in a small saucepan and heat until steaming but not boiling. Maintain the steaming-hot state over low heat for 30 minutes, taking care not to allow the mixture to boil.
2. Pour into small teacups and enjoy.

Serves 4

·ɔ[MULLED CIDER 🥄🥄🥄]ɔ··

To make the mulled cider, substitute 2 cups apple cider for the wine and reduce the honey to 1 tablespoon.

·ɔ[PLUMPTREE'S VITAMINIZED NERVE FOOD (HEALTH BARS)]ɔ··

Dr. Plumptree had a thing or two going for him with these delicious whole-grain, high-protein chewy health bars. They're so delicious you would never know they're good for you too.

1 cup ground nuts, such as pecans, walnuts, or almonds

1 cup nonfat milk powder

½ teaspoon salt

½ teaspoon baking soda

2 cups rolled oats (old-fashioned, not quick-cooking)

1 cup shredded sweetened coconut

1 cup golden raisins

1 cup chopped nuts, such as pecans, walnuts, or almonds

1 cup light brown sugar

16 tablespoons (1 cup) butter, at room temperature

2 large eggs, at room temperature

¼ cup honey

1 tablespoon pure vanilla extract

1. Adjust the oven rack to the middle position and preheat the oven to 350°F. Line a rimmed baking sheet with heavy-duty aluminum foil, allowing the foil to come up the sides for easy removal. Spray the foil with baking spray.

2. In a mixing bowl, whisk together the ground nuts, milk powder, salt, and baking soda. In another mixing bowl, combine the oats, coconut, golden raisins, and chopped nuts. In a third mixing bowl, using an electric mixer, beat the brown sugar and butter until light and fluffy, scraping down the sides as needed, about 5 minutes.

3. Add the eggs one at a time to the brown sugar–butter mixture, beating after each until incorporated. Add the honey and vanilla and beat until combined. Add the ground nut mixture, mixing on the slowest speed until combined. Add the oats mixture, mixing on the slowest speed until combined. Scrape the mixture into the prepared pan. Grasp the aluminum foil at one end to

prevent sliding, then spread the mixture to the edges and smooth the top with a rubber spatula.

4. Bake for 25 minutes, rotating the pan halfway through baking, until evenly golden brown. Cool completely in the pan.

5. To cut, remove the foil from the pan and peel away the edges of the foil from the bars. Using a sharp chef's knife, make 7 slices along the length and 5 slices along the width to make 48 squares.

Makes 4 dozen

·ᴣ[WHOLEMEAL SUGAR BISCUITS 𝄢𝄢𝄢]ᴤ·

In the UK, the word *biscuit* means "cookie," and *wholemeal* means "whole grain." For long voyages on ships, bakers made biscuits from a stiff dough, baked them in a loaf, then sliced and baked them again to make sure they would store well. That doesn't sound very appealing, but I'm sure in Narnia, you could take cookies on long voyages without worrying about spoilage—otherwise, what's the point of being in a fantasy world?

1½ cups white whole-wheat flour (see sidebar)
1½ cups all-purpose flour
¾ teaspoon baking soda
½ teaspoon salt
16 tablespoons (1 cup) butter, at room temperature

1 cup granulated sugar
2 large eggs, at room temperature
2 teaspoons pure vanilla extract
1 egg, beaten with 1 tablespoon water
Turbinado sugar or granulated sugar for sprinkling

1. Adjust the oven racks to the upper and lower middle positions. Preheat the oven to 350°F and line 2 baking sheets with parchment paper. Whisk the flours, baking soda, and salt in a large mixing bowl.

2. In a separate bowl, beat the butter and granulated sugar until light and fluffy, scraping down the sides as needed, about 5 minutes. Add the eggs, one at a time, beating after each until incorporated. Add the vanilla and beat until combined. Add the flour mixture and mix on the slowest speed until combined.

3. Divide the dough in half. Working with one half at a time, roll out the dough on a floured work surface to ¼-inch thick and stamp out rounds of dough with a 1½-inch cookie cutter. Lay the cookies ½ inch apart on the cookie sheets. Brush with the beaten egg and sprinkle with sugar.

4. Bake for 10 minutes, rotating and switching the pans halfway through the baking time. The cookies will be pale but should look dry.

Makes 8 to 9 dozen

White whole-wheat flour contains the same nutrients as regular whole-wheat flour but has a lighter color and texture. It can be found in the baking aisle of the grocery store.

Packing for the Road with Puddleglum

· *Wholemeal Lemon–Ginger Biscuits with Almonds* ·*Bacon* ·*Eel Stew* ·

Puddleglum is my favorite character. I simply could not help falling in love with this gloom-and-doom but kindhearted soul. Imagine what the other Marsh-wiggles must be like, if, according to Puddleglum, they think he doesn't "take life seriously enough" and that he's "altogether too full of bobance and bounce and high spirits." Nevertheless, this brave character packs up food for the children and leads them on their quest (*The Silver Chair*, chapter 5). Use the following recipes and the crispy bacon recipe from the "Breakfast for the Man-Stomach of Centaurs" menu on page 23 to take along on your quest

·❧⟦ WHOLEMEAL LEMON-GINGER BISCUITS WITH ALMONDS ❘❘❘⟧⟨·

Ginger biscuits take a hallowed place in British history, so much so that they take up a whole entry to themselves in *The Oxford Companion to Food* (not even chocolate-chip cookies merit that distinction). Usually, ginger biscuits refer to ginger snaps, but this recipe offers a softer, chewier version.

2 cups all-purpose flour

1½ cups white whole-wheat flour
  (see note on page 72)

¾ teaspoon baking soda

1 teaspoon baking powder

½ teaspoon salt

1 tablespoon ground ginger

16 tablespoons (1 cup) butter, at room temperature

½ cup granulated sugar

½ cup dark brown sugar

Grated zest of 1 lemon

2 large eggs, at room temperature

¼ cup light corn syrup or golden syrup

Juice of 1 lemon

1 cup chopped almonds

1. Adjust the oven racks to the upper and lower middle positions and preheat the oven to 375°F. Line 2 cookie sheets with parchment paper.

2. In a large mixing bowl, whisk together the flours, baking soda, baking powder, salt, and ginger. In a separate bowl, using an electric mixer, beat the butter, granulated sugar, brown sugar, and lemon zest until light and fluffy, scraping down the sides as needed, about 5 minutes.

3. Add the eggs one at a time, beating after each until incorporated. Add the corn syrup or golden syrup and lemon juice and beat until combined. Add the flour mixture and mix on the slowest speed until combined. Stir in the chopped almonds.

4. Drop the dough by heaping tablespoonfuls 2 inches apart on the prepared cookie sheets, or use a medium cookie scoop to portion the dough. Bake for 10 minutes, switching and rotating the pans halfway through baking. Remove to wire racks to cool. Repeat until cookie dough is used up.

5. You will need to remove the cookies against your better judgment, as they will look underbaked. They will set up as they cool. They will be pale but should look dry. Do not overbake, as they will turn hard when they cool.

Makes 4 dozen

⋯⊰❡ Bacon ❡⊱⋯

Use the crispy bacon recipe from the "Breakfast for the Man-Stomach of Centaurs" menu on page 23.

⋯⊰❡ Eel Stew 🥄🥄🥄 ❡⊱⋯

THANKS TO CHEF CHRIS KOCH FOR THIS RECIPE.

Did you know that eels like fresh peas? They slip out of the water sometimes and into nearby fields to snack on this delicacy.

2 pounds eel, cleaned; head, tail, and fins (wings) removed

1 teaspoon sea salt

¼ teaspoon freshly ground white pepper

2 cups all-purpose flour

½ cup vegetable oil

¾ cup red wine vinegar

1½ cups clam juice or seafood stock

1 cup white wine

½ cup olive oil

1 pound carrots, peeled and cut into
½-inch pieces

1 cup yellow onion, peeled and chopped

Salt, to taste

Freshly ground white pepper, to taste

1. Cut the eel crosswise into 3-inch-thick pieces. Season with the sea salt and pepper. Place the flour in a resealable plastic bag. Add the eel to the bag, shake to coat, and then shake off excess flour.

2. Heat the vegetable oil in a large, wide, heavy pan over medium-high heat. Add the eel in a single layer and cook until lightly browned, turning once, about 5 minutes per side. Transfer the eel to paper towels to drain. Discard the oil and wipe out the pan.

3. Combine the vinegar, clam juice or seafood stock, and wine in a medium pot and bring to a simmer over medium heat. Turn off the heat and move the pan to the side. Do not continue simmering. Reserve the stewing liquid.

4. Meanwhile, heat the olive oil over medium-high heat in the same pan used to brown the eel. Add the carrots and onions and cook, stirring often, until lightly browned, about 7 minutes. Stir in ½ cup stewing liquid; simmer briefly, stirring and scraping up any brown bits stuck to the bottom of the pan for about 1 minute more.

5. Stir in the remaining stewing liquid. Bring to a boil and let boil for 10 minutes to reduce the volume; then arrange the eel in the sauce. Cook until the eel easily pulls away from the bone, about 10 minutes, occasionally stirring the sauce and shaking the pan gently so as not to break the eel pieces. The eel should be tender and the sauce should be velvety and emulsified. Season with the salt and pepper.

Serves 6

SNACK SUGGESTED
BY A GIANTESS

· Posset ·Sugared Almonds and Caraway Comfits ·

The giantess queen doesn't care at all about Jill's comfort; she just doesn't want to hear her crying. She also wants Jill nicely fattened up for the Autumn Feast, and what better way to do that than with sugary foods? So she orders her servants to take Jill away and give her toys and sweets—and dolls, which Jill finds insulting (*The Silver Chair*, chapter 8).

⸙ POSSET ⸙

Of course, posset is unsuitable for a child, but the giantess is not disturbed by the alcohol content. Posset is an old-fashioned drink that many thought was a good tonic for an invalid or to cure illness. It was made by curdling milk with wine or ale; then it was sweetened and spiced and served warm. Many richer versions with cream and nuts were made to serve as desserts. In these versions, breadcrumbs were also added to make the possets thick enough to eat with a spoon; they were then called "eating possets." Although I found this drink unusual, to say the least, I also found it oddly comforting and satisfying. Today, the word *posset* survives in a British dessert called lemon posset.

POSSET—FOR ADULTS ONLY! ♩♩♩

3 cups whole milk	⅛ teaspoon ground cloves
½ cup sugar	⅛ teaspoon ground allspice
1 teaspoon ground cinnamon	4 large egg yolks
¼ teaspoon ground nutmeg	1 cup dry white sherry or ale

I. Heat the milk, sugar, and spices in a medium saucepan, stirring to dissolve. Do not boil.

2. Place the egg yolks in a mixing bowl. Temper the egg yolks by adding 1 cup of the hot milk mixture into the yolks while whisking constantly. Then pour the yolk mixture into the pan, stirring constantly over medium heat until the mixture has thickened and is hot and steaming but not bubbling, about 5 minutes.

3. Pour the mixture through a sieve and return to the saucepan. Stir in the sherry or ale and pour immediately into 4 or 5 mugs.

4. To eat, spoon up the curds and then drink the alcoholic whey that has settled to the bottom.

Serves 4 to 5

LEMON POSSET FOR KIDS ♪♪♪

*4 large egg whites, at room
    temperature (see sidebar)*
½ cup granulated sugar
Juice of 1 lemon

1 cup heavy cream
Grated zest of 1 lemon
½ cup confectioners' sugar

1. In a mixing bowl, whip the egg whites, sugar, and lemon juice until stiff and glossy. In a separate bowl, whip the heavy cream with the lemon zest and confectioners' sugar until stiff peaks form.

2. Fold the 2 mixtures together in a large mixing bowl. Scoop into dessert bowls or crystal glasses and serve with sugar cookies, if desired. The mixture can also be frozen and served as an ice cream.

Makes about 2 quarts

> This dessert contains raw eggs. To reduce the risk of contamination, use fresh eggs that have no cracks in the shells. If you are still concerned, you can use egg white powder in place of the fresh eggs. Follow the manufacturer's instructions for making beaten egg whites.

·❧ SUGARED ALMONDS AND CARAWAY COMFITS ♪♪♪ ❧·

Comfit is the name given to a sweet made by coating a nut or seed with many layers of sugar. These treats were popular in medieval times and into the nineteenth century. Queen Elizabeth I was especially fond of caraway comfits, also called "kissing comfits" because they were perfumed to sweeten the breath. She ate so many sweets, her teeth rotted.

Fortunately, with modern dental hygiene, you can safely eat these, as long as you brush and floss regularly.

Today, candy manufacturers make comfits with a piece of equipment called a panning machine. Panning by hand is, I must warn you, tedious work that will not give as smooth a coating as a machine will. It requires a lot of practice to get the technique right, and even after lots of attempts, I wasn't quite successful with the caraways, though I had an easier time with the almonds. This method is similar to the one used in Queen Elizabeth's time. The almonds and caraways are made the same way, so here is the recipe for both:

1 cup sugar　　　　　　　　　　*10 almonds or 1 teaspoon caraway*
¼ cup water　　　　　　　　　　*seeds*

1.　Place the sugar and water in a small saucepan and bring to a boil while stirring. Wash down the sides of the pan with a pastry brush dipped in hot water. Clip a candy thermometer to the pan and cook, without stirring, until the sugar reaches 238°F. Reduce heat to the lowest setting and let the mixture cool slightly for about 10 minutes.

2.　Place the almonds or caraway seeds in a small pan. You can work on an unheated burner next to the pan of syrup. Drizzle a small amount of the sugar syrup (about 1 teaspoon for the almonds or a few drops for the caraway seeds) over the almonds or caraway seeds. Wearing a heavy rubber glove on your right hand, place your right hand into the pan and turn the pan with your left hand, round and round, while pressing down on the almonds or seeds, until the sugar crystallizes and the almonds or seeds stop sticking to each other. This is called the first charge. Charge the almonds or seeds with the sugar syrup 8 to 10 times or until the almond or seed is covered with a thin coat. Don't worry if the coat isn't perfectly even.

3.　Place the almonds or seeds on a baking sheet lined with parchment paper. Place the baking sheet in the oven and turn the oven on to its lowest setting; 170°F is best (do not preheat). Keep the oven on for 30 minutes, then turn it off and let the oven cool without opening the door. This process dries the sugar coating as well as whitens it.

4.　Repeat this process 2 or more times, giving 8 to 10 charges and drying in the oven each time. How many times you repeat this process depends on how thick you want the coating to be. You will need to wash down the sides of the pan and reheat the sugar to the correct temperature each time. You may also need to clean the pan for coating the comfits between each repetition. If you want to create a lot of layers, you can prepare as many fresh batches of syrup as needed.

Makes about 10 sugared almonds and a handful of caraway comfits

MARCHING TOWARD THE LAST BATTLE

· Battle Biscuits ·

In preparation for battle, Tirian, the children, and their companions first remove their Calormene disguises, so as not to be taken for the enemy. Unfortunately, the only provisions they can salvage are some biscuits (*The Last Battle*, chapter 8).

⋯⊰[BATTLE BISCUITS ⸙⸙⸙]⊱⋯

These are the biscuits you'd want to take with you into battle. Their high protein content will keep your hunger at bay longer than ordinary biscuits will.

2 cups all-purpose flour
1 cup finely ground almonds
1 cup nonfat milk powder
1 teaspoon baking soda
½ teaspoon salt

2 teaspoons ground cardamom
16 tablespoons (1 cup) butter, at
*   room temperature*
1 cup sugar
2 large eggs, at room temperature

1. Adjust the oven racks to the upper and lower middle positions and preheat the oven to 350°F. Line 2 cookie sheets with parchment paper.

2. In a large mixing bowl, whisk together the flour, ground almonds, powdered milk, baking soda, salt, and cardamom. In a separate bowl, using an electric mixer, beat the butter and sugar until light and fluffy, scraping down the sides as needed, about 5 minutes. Add the eggs, one a time, to the butter-sugar mixture, beating after each until incorporated. Add the flour mixture and mix on the slowest speed until incorporated, scraping down the sides as needed.

3. Divide the dough in half. Working with one half at a time, roll out the dough on a floured work surface to ¼-inch thickness and cut out circles with a 2½-inch cookie cutter. Place the biscuits ½ inch apart on the cookie sheets. The biscuit

dough can be rerolled as needed. Bake 10 minutes, rotating and switching the sheets halfway through baking, until light golden brown on the bottom (tops should be pale). Repeat with the remaining dough.

Makes about 7 dozen biscuits

Variations

The biscuits can be flavored differently if cardamom is not available. For spice biscuits, replace the cardamom with 1½ teaspoons ground cinnamon, ½ teaspoon ground nutmeg, and ¼ teaspoon ground cloves. For cinnamon biscuits, replace the cardamom with 2 teaspoons ground cinnamon. For ginger biscuits, replace the cardamom with 1 tablespoon ground ginger. For vanilla biscuits, omit the cardamom and add 2 teaspoons pure vanilla extract after adding the eggs to the butter-sugar mixture. For orange or lemon biscuits, omit the cardamom; beat the butter and sugar with the grated zest of 1 orange or lemon, and add 1 teaspoon orange or lemon extract after adding the eggs to the butter-sugar mixture, if desired. The variations are endless, and you can make up your own!

On the Way to the Queen of the Deep Realm

· Flat, Flabby Cakes (Brown Sugar—Cinnamon Pancakes) ·

The warden tells Puddleglum, Jill, and Eustace that few people who board his ship ever return to the Overworld. With these daunting words, the three huddle together on the cold, dark, cheerless ship that will bring them to the Queen of the Deep Realm, fearing what awaits them. They are fed "flat, flabby cakes," and they pass the time sleeping, waking, eating, sleeping, waking, eating...it's a dreary time (*The Silver Chair*, chapter 10).

﹃ FLAT, FLABBY CAKES (BROWN SUGAR—CINNAMON PANCAKES) ﹄

I had to do a bit of thinking to figure out what these flat, flabby cakes may have been. And then I realized that this could be an unflattering description of pancakes! It's all a question of perspective: one person can look at a pancake and see a soft, thick, yummy breakfast food; another could look at it and see a fat, flabby cake that you would rather give to your dog. Pancakes have a long history; they were a useful way for housewives to use up their butter, cream, and eggs before Lent.

This recipe results in pancakes so moist and sweet, they need no accompaniment of butter or syrup, and thus can be taken aboard cheerless ships to meet fearsome queens.

1 cup all-purpose flour
1 teaspoon baking soda
1 teaspoon baking powder
1 teaspoon ground cinnamon
¼ teaspoon salt

1 cup buttermilk, at room
  temperature (see sidebar)
1 large egg, at room temperature
6 tablespoons butter, melted and
  cooled somewhat
⅓ cup dark brown sugar

1. Whisk the flour, baking soda, baking powder, cinnamon, and salt in a large mixing bowl. In a separate bowl, whisk together the buttermilk, egg, butter, and brown sugar until smooth. Pour the buttermilk mixture into the flour mixture and fold the mixtures together with a wooden spoon or rubber spatula just until moistened. Do not overmix, or the pancakes will be tough rather than tender. The batter should be lumpy.

2. Cook the pancakes on a hot greased griddle or skillet, using about ¼ cup batter for each cake. Cook over medium heat until golden brown, 3 to 4 minutes per side. Watch the heat carefully; due to these pancakes' high sugar content, they can scorch easily.

Makes about 1 dozen pancakes

Instead of the buttermilk, you can use 1 cup milk mixed with 1 tablespoon lemon juice and let it stand 10 minutes until it curdles. (Or you can heat briefly in the microwave, about 30 to 60 seconds.)

CHAPTER THREE
LUNCH AND DINNER MENUS

The characters in The Chronicles of Narnia enjoy three meals a day, but the entrenched concept of three square meals is fairly modern. Two meals a day, a morning breakfast and afternoon dinner—with perhaps just a light snack in between called luncheon, nuncheon, or bever, or a light meal after dinner called supper— were the norm until the nineteenth century, when dinner was gradually pushed to later in the day. Lunch was mostly a meal for women and children, while the men ate a huge meal in the morning before going off to work and another huge one when they came home.

Needless to say, I am very happy about the development of lunch, and working men who take it for granted should be grateful too. Although I suppose a full English fry-up in the morning could probably keep you going for several days without eating.

One of my favorite things about The Chronicles of Narnia (besides C. S. Lewis's captivating story and storytelling style) is the number of meals and amount of food the characters consume. It's a lot of fun to read about their lunches and dinners and what they ate; C. S. Lewis obviously enjoyed food and wrote about it with such gusto that it makes your mouth water just to read about it. This is why I'm sure you'll enjoy preparing these delicious meals as much I enjoyed developing them.

British cooking is the style that most frequently appears in The Chronicles of Narnia (although there are some examples of Mediterranean cuisine in the series, from the Calormenes and Telmarines). While I was conducting my research on British cooking, I learned that British cuisine does not deserve its negative reputation. A tradition of good home cooking does exist in the UK. As you'll see from the recipes that follow, the British have some wonderful dishes up their sleeves. Most of these dishes require pantry staples or items typically found in your local grocery store, so you don't have to search specialty food stores to prepare these foods.

Dinner in Those Days

First Course
· Vermicelli Soup · Lobster Rissoles ·
· Pan–Seared Portobello Mushroom Caps ·

Second Course
· Braised Beef with Velvet Gravy ·
· Roast Duck with Sage and Onion Stuffing ·
· Green Peas with Sweet Butter · Mashed Turnips ·

Desserts
· Charlotte Russe · Baked Batter Fruit Pudding ·

The first sentence in *The Magician's Nephew* states, "This is a story about something that happened long ago when your grandfather was a child." If you had been a child in England in the 1950s when this book was published, then your grandfather would have been a child during the end of Queen Victoria's reign. In his description of the time period, Lewis writes that "meals were nicer." And so they were. In fact, that is an understatement. Victorian dinners were lavish and extravagant in the extreme, so much so that the menu that follows, while appearing large to our modern tastes, is pygmy-sized by Victorian standards (*The Magician's Nephew*, chapter 1).

To give you an idea of a typical Victorian menu, try this one from *Mrs. Beeton's Book of Household Management*:

> *DINNER FOR 12 PERSONS (January). FIRST COURSE. Carrot Soup à la Crécy. Oxtail Soup. Turbot and Lobster Sauce. Fried Smelts, with Dutch Sauce. ENTREES. Mutton Cutlets, with Soubise Sauce. Sweetbreads. Oyster Patties. Fillets of Rabbits. SECOND COURSE. Roast Turkey. Stewed Rump of Beef à la Jardinière. Boiled Ham, garnished with Brussels Sprouts. Boiled Chickens and Celery Sauce. THIRD COURSE. Roast Hare. Teal. Eggs à la Neige. Vol-au-Vent of Preserved Fruit. 1 Jelly. 1 Cream. Potatoes à la Maître d'Hôtel. Grilled Mushrooms. DESSERT AND ICES [not listed].*

Lest you say, "Well, that's a dinner party for twelve; of course it's huge," then take a look at a sample menu from "plain family dinners for January" also from Mrs. Beeton's cookbook. This is for Monday:

> *"1. The remains of turbot [from yesterday's dinner] warmed in oyster sauce, potatoes. 2. Cold pork, stewed steak. 3. Open jam tart, which should have been made with the pieces of paste left from the damson tart [for yesterday's dinner]; baked arrowroot pudding."*

It's like feasting every day! I'm getting a time machine and going back to Victorian England!

ᐧᐧᓂ VERMICELLI SOUP 🥄🥄🥄 ᓂᐧᐧ

Vermicelli means "little worms"; it's like spaghetti, but thinner. Historians have a hard time pinning down when pasta was invented because references to pasta-like products appear as early as Greek and Roman times, and it's not clear if these doughs were dried and then boiled. The Jerusalem Talmud (written in the fifth century) discusses whether boiled dough may be eaten on Passover, when eating leavened bread is forbidden. Certainly, quite a lot of recipes that used macaroni and other pasta products can be found in old British cookbooks.

*2½ pounds beef with bones, such as
    neck bones (any cheap cut with
    bones attached will do)*
*1 onion, cut in half from pole to pole
    and sliced*
1 tablespoon peppercorns
2 carrots, peeled and cut into chunks
2 celery ribs, cut into chunks

1 parsnip, peeled and cut into chunks
1 turnip, peeled and cut into chunks
1 fresh sprig rosemary
2 sage leaves
A few sprigs parsley
Salt, to taste
*2 cups cooked vermicelli or thin egg
    noodles*

1. Spray a Dutch oven or large, wide pot with cooking spray. Sear the meat over high heat on both sides until crusty brown, 3 to 4 minutes per side. If the cut of beef is too large to fit in the pot all at once, it's only necessary to sear one batch; that will create enough browning to flavor the stock. Transfer the meat to a large plate.

2. Reduce the heat to medium-high and add the onion and just a little water, about ¼ cup, to deglaze the pot. Cook, stirring frequently, until the water has evaporated and the onions have started to brown. Add the meat back to the pot along with any accumulated juices and fill with water up to within 2 inches of the rim.

3. Bring to a simmer, reduce the heat to low, and keep at a simmer for 2½ hours, skimming the scum and fat off the surface every so often as it rises. Try not to let the pot boil, as boiling will make the finished stock cloudy.

4. Add the peppercorns, carrots, celery, parsnip, turnip, rosemary, sage, and parsley and simmer for 1 more hour. Strain the soup through a fine-mesh

sieve and discard the solids. Taste the soup and adjust with salt accordingly. Use
1½ quarts (6 cups) for the vermicelli. If you don't have that much broth, your
stock has become extra concentrated, so just add water to reach 6 cups. If you
have more than 6 cups, measure out the 6 cups and reserve the remaining stock
to add to a soup or a stew. Stir the vermicelli into the measured stock.

5. Divide the soup among 6 bowls.

Serves 6

···⊲[LOBSTER RISSOLES 🥄🥄🥄]⊳···

A *rissole* is a French word for puff pastry filled with ground meat or fish
and then fried.

THANKS TO CHEF CHRIS KOCH FOR THIS RECIPE.

1 cup chopped onions	*¼ cup flour*
½ cup chopped celery	*1 cup heavy cream*
½ cup chopped carrots	*Salt, to taste*
3 cups water	*Freshly ground black pepper, to taste*
1 cup dry white wine	*2 sheets frozen puff pastry, thawed*
2 lobsters, live	*1 quart vegetable oil for deep frying*
4 tablespoons butter	*½ cup fresh flat-leaf parsley leaves*

1. Place the onions, celery, and carrots into a 4-quart pot. Add the water and
    wine, bring to a boil, and reduce to low heat; simmer for 15 minutes. While the
    vegetables cook, remove the meat from the tail and claws of each lobster (see the
    sidebar). Chop the meat and set aside. Place the shells and body of the lobster
    into the cooking pot. Simmer for 30 minutes and strain; discard the vegetables
    and shells. Reserve the cooking liquid.

2. Wipe out the pot and return the cooking liquid to the pot. Bring to a boil and
    cook to reduce the amount to 2 cups. Strain again and set aside.

3. In a medium saucepan, melt the butter over medium-high heat. Once the
    butter is melted, add the flour all at once and stir with a whisk for 2 minutes.
    Slowly whisk in the reserved cooking liquid and cook for 10 minutes, whisking
    slowly to create a very thick sauce. Reduce the heat to low and simmer for 15

minutes, taking care not to scorch the sauce. Add the chopped lobster to the sauce, stir, and remove from the heat.

4. Dust a work surface with flour. Place a sheet of the puff pastry on the dusted work surface and dust the top of the puff pastry with more flour. Lightly roll the sheet out to a 12-inch square. Cut four 6-inch circles from the sheet and set aside. Repeat with the second sheet.

5. Lay the circles on the work surface and divide the lobster and sauce among the circles, placing the mixture in the center of each circle. Brush the edges of each circle with water. Close the edges by bringing one side of dough over and pressing it along the edges. Press to remove excess air and crimp the edges with a fork to seal.

6. Place 2 inches of vegetable oil in a pot at least 6 inches deep, or use a deep fryer. Heat the oil to 350°F or until the oil bubbles when you dip the edge of a rissole into it. Fry in batches until golden brown and drain on paper towels.

7. Once all the rissoles are fried, add the parsley to the oil and fry until all the bubbles are gone. Serve 2 rissoles per person and garnish with fried parsley.

Serves 4

To remove the meat from the lobster, lay the lobster on a cutting board. Place the tip of a chef's knife on the head of the lobster and strike the butt of the knife, driving the blade through the lobster to the cutting board. To remove the meat from the tail, cut the tail lengthwise in half and work your fingers between the meat and the shell to remove. To remove the meat from the claws, crack with a mallet or other heavy object and remove the meat.

⊶ Braised Beef with Velvet Gravy 𝄞𝄞𝄞 ⊷

So famed are the British for their superb skills at roasting beef that the French nickname for them used to be *rosbifs*, French for *roast beef.*

1 (4-pound) chuck eye roast
2 tablespoons vegetable oil
1 onion, chopped
2 celery ribs, chopped
2 medium carrots, chopped
10 ounces mushrooms, sliced
3 garlic cloves, minced

2 tablespoons all-purpose flour
2 cups beef broth
½ teaspoon dried sage
½ teaspoon dried thyme
Salt, to taste
Freshly ground black pepper, to taste

1. Spray a large, wide pot (such as a Dutch oven) with cooking spray. Sear the roast over high heat on both sides until crusty brown, 3 to 5 minutes per side. Transfer to a large plate.

2. Reduce the heat to medium-high and add the oil. Add the onion, celery, carrots, and mushrooms and cook, stirring to scrape up the flavorful browned bits on the bottom of the pot. Raise the heat to high and cook, stirring occasionally, until the water cooks out, about 5 minutes. Continue to cook, stirring frequently, until the vegetable mixture browns. Add the garlic and stir until fragrant, a few seconds.

3. Sprinkle the flour over the mixture and stir to combine. Pour in the broth and stir until smooth. Add the sage, thyme, salt, and pepper. (If the broth is salty, you may not need to add salt at all, so taste it first).

4. Place the roast back into the pot, along with the accumulated juices. Reduce the heat to low, cover, and simmer for 3 hours.

5. Remove the roast to a cutting board and cover with aluminum foil. Allow to rest for at least 20 minutes before slicing. Slice thinly against the grain.

6. While the roast is resting, pour the gravy into a food processor and process until smooth. Push through a sieve into a bowl, scraping and pressing to extract as much liquid as possible. Lay the meat slices on a platter and drizzle with the gravy. Pass extra gravy on the side.

Serves 6 to 8

·◈ ROAST DUCK WITH SAGE AND ONION STUFFING ♪♪♪ ◈·

Isabella Beeton (1836–1865) is my go-to resource on all foods Victorian. By age twenty-five, this brilliant and productive woman had published a massive tome called *Mrs. Beeton's Book of Household Management*. Besides containing hundreds of recipes, this famous manual also includes instructions on how to manage and keep a Victorian household (including managing the servants), Victorian cures and remedies, and rules of etiquette for dinner parties and other social events. So it's no wonder I rely heavily on her for my research of traditional British food. No doubt, C. S. Lewis enjoyed many of the dishes that she famously wrote recipes for. The following recipe is an updated version of Mrs. Beeton's.

For this recipe, you need to roast the duck and bake the stuffing separately. Stuffing the cavity of the duck prevents the heat from circulating properly, leaving parts of the duck overcooked and others undercooked.

Roast Duck

1 (4- to 5-pound) duck
Salt, for sprinkling

Freshly ground black pepper, for
  sprinkling
2 cups water

1. Preheat the oven to 450°F. Remove the giblets and neck from the duck's cavity and sprinkle the duck evenly with the salt and pepper. Place the duck on a V-shaped roasting rack set in a roasting pan. Pierce the skin in several places with a fork or the tip of a knife to allow the fat to drain.

2. Roast for 30 minutes, then reduce the temperature to 325°F. Continue roasting until the duck registers 165°F on a meat thermometer, about another 1½ hours.

3. Remove from the oven and tip the duck slightly to drain the juices from the cavity. Allow to rest 20 minutes before carving.

4. Carve at the table, placing a serving of stuffing next to each piece of duck.

Sage and Onion Stuffing

12 ounces (about 6 cups) fresh
  breadcrumbs (made from about
  10 slices sandwich bread; no need
  to remove crusts unless they are
  very tough)
2 onions

2 tablespoons vegetable oil
2 large eggs
10 fresh sage leaves
½ teaspoon salt
¼ teaspoon freshly ground black
  pepper

1. Set the oven rack to the middle position and preheat the oven to 350°F. Spray a 4½-by-8½-inch or similar size loaf pan with baking spray with flour and set aside. Place the breadcrumbs in a large mixing bowl.

2. Chop one and a half of the onions and cut the remaining half into chunks. Heat the oil in a skillet and add the chopped onions. Cook over high heat, stirring frequently, until well browned, about 10 minutes.

3. Place the remaining onion chunks in a food processor and process until it resembles the consistency of applesauce, scraping down the sides as needed. Add the eggs, sage leaves, salt, and pepper and process until smooth. Add the egg-onion-sage mixture and the sautéed onions to the breadcrumbs and mix until thoroughly combined. Scrape the stuffing into the prepared loaf pan, smooth the top, cover with aluminum foil, and bake for 1 hour or until set.

Serves 4, with extra stuffing

·ᗕ[green peas with butter *♪♪♪*]ᗒ·

Unless you have peas growing in your garden, your best bet is to go with frozen. Unlike other fresh vegetables, peas must be eaten within hours of being picked, as they begin to degrade right away. Frozen peas, which are frozen immediately after harvesting, will taste fresher and brighter than the "fresh" ones in the produce section of your local supermarket.

1 pound frozen peas	*Salt, to taste*
2 tablespoons butter	*Freshly ground black pepper, to taste*

1. Place the peas in a pot and add just enough water to cover the peas. Bring to a boil, then reduce the heat to medium and simmer until crisp-tender and bright green, about 5 to 7 minutes. Drain the peas and return to the pot.
2. Add the butter, salt, and pepper and toss until the butter is melted and the ingredients are combined.

Serves 4 to 6

·ᗕ[mashed turnips *♪♪♪*]ᗒ·

The Samnites, who vainly resisted joining the Roman empire, offered Roman hero Curius Dentatus lots of riches to fight with them. Dentatus was roasting turnips when the offer came. Being a loyal and true Roman, he refused the Samnite ambassador's offer and turned his attention back to his turnips. Cultures around the world have been cooking and eating turnips since 2000 BC, in ancient China as well as Rome. There are many ways to prepare this vegetable, which comes in several varieties, but the common British preparation is to boil turnips—and then sometimes to mash them. If you add mashed potatoes, chopped chives, and butter to the mashed turnips, you get a Scottish dish called *clapshot* (the Scots call turnips *neeps*).

3 pounds turnips (about 3 large
or 5 medium), peeled and cut
into chunks

1 tablespoon butter
Salt, to taste
Freshly ground black pepper, to taste

1. Place the turnips in a large pot and cover with water. Bring to a boil. Cover and reduce the heat to medium. Cook, boiling gently, until the turnips are very soft, about 45 minutes.

2. Drain the turnips in a colander. Line a bowl with paper towels, dump the turnips in, and cover with several layers of paper towels. Using silicone oven mitts so as not to burn your hands, press down to extract as much water as possible. Discard the paper towels, turn the neeps out onto a plate, and peel off the remaining paper towels. Line the bowl with paper towels again and repeat the whole process 2 or 3 more times, until most of the water has been extracted.

3. Push the turnips through a sieve using a wooden spoon. This is the tedious part! It removes the fibrous parts of the turnips. You can skip this step and simply mash the turnips, if desired.

4. Return the neeps to the pot, add the butter, and stir until heated through and the butter is melted. Season with the salt and pepper and serve.

Makes 4 rather small servings

⋅⊰[CHARLOTTE RUSSE ♪♪♪]⊱⋅

The original charlotte, the apple charlotte, was named for Queen Charlotte (consort to King George III) because of her support of apple growers. But it was the famous French chef Marie-Antoine Carême who elevated this dessert into the fancy confection known as *charlotte russe*.

If this dessert is too involved for you, the only shortcut I can offer is to buy pound cake or angel food cake instead of making the sponge cake.

1 sponge cake, homemade or store bought (recipe follows)
¼ cup currant or strawberry jelly (not jam), melted

1 recipe Vanilla Mousse (recipe follows)
1 recipe Whipped Cream Frosting (recipe follows) or 2 cups store-bought whipped cream frosting

1. Line a 2½–quart bowl with plastic wrap. Cut ½-inch wide strips of cake long enough to fit from one side of the bowl to the other (the exact length and width don't really matter). Lay about 3 strips, depending on size, along one length of the bowl. Line the other 2 empty sides with shorter strips of cake. Use scraps to fill in any empty spaces.

2. Brush the melted currant or strawberry jelly over the cake, giving it a few coats of jelly. Fill the inside with the vanilla mousse (you may have a bit left over, but is that ever a problem?). Cover the mousse with scraps of cake and then cover with plastic wrap. Refrigerate until the mousse is set.

3. To remove and frost the charlotte, tug on the plastic wrap to loosen it. Invert the bowl onto a large plate and remove the bowl and plastic wrap. Cover the charlotte with the frosting. This keeps in the refrigerator for several days.

Serves 6 to 8

SPONGE CAKE

1 cup cake flour
1 teaspoon baking powder
¼ teaspoon salt
6 large eggs, separated, at room temperature

1 cup sugar, divided
¼ teaspoon cream of tartar
1 teaspoon pure vanilla extract
½ cup vegetable oil

1. Set the oven rack to the middle position and preheat the oven to 350°F. Grease a half–sheet cake pan and line it with parchment paper.

2. Sift the flour, baking powder, and salt onto a separate piece of parchment paper. In a large mixing bowl, using an electric mixer, whip the egg whites with ½ cup of the sugar, the cream of tartar, and the vanilla until stiff peaks form. In a separate mixing

bowl, whip the egg yolks with the remaining sugar until thick and lemon-colored, 5 to 10 minutes. Drizzle in the oil a little at a time, beating after each addition until incorporated and scraping down the sides as needed. This will take a few minutes.

3. Add the flour mixture to the yolk mixture and stir until incorporated, scraping down the sides as needed. Whisk in a quarter of the beaten egg whites to lighten the mixture. Fold in half the remaining egg whites, mixing gently until incorporated, then fold in the other half. Scrape the batter into the prepared pan. Bake for 25 to 30 minutes, rotating the pan halfway through baking, until golden and the cake feels set when touched lightly in the center.

4. Cool completely in the pan. Cover and store until ready to use, up to 4 days at room temperature. If the edges are hard, they will soften after a day or two if well covered. Run a knife along the edges before inverting the cake to remove it from the pan.

VANILLA MOUSSE

¼ cup water
1 envelope (1 tablespoon) gelatin
4 large egg whites, at room
*   temperature*

¾ cup sugar, divided
¼ teaspoon salt
1 cup heavy cream
1 teaspoon pure vanilla extract

1. Sprinkle the gelatin over the water and allow to soften. Microwave for 30 seconds, whisk to dissolve, and set aside to cool.

2. Whip the egg whites with ½ cup of the sugar and the salt until stiff peaks form. Whisk in the gelatin mixture.

3. In a separate mixing bowl, whip the heavy cream with the remaining ¼ cup of sugar and the vanilla until stiff peaks form. Fold the 2 mixtures together.

You can make the cake a day or two before assembling the charlotte, but not the mousse. It will set in the fridge and will be impossible to work with. Make the mousse right before assembly.

WHIPPED CREAM FROSTING

1 cup heavy cream
⅓ cup confectioners' sugar

1 teaspoon pure vanilla extract

1. Whip all the ingredients together until stiff peaks form.

·◦❧ BAKED BATTER FRUIT PUDDING 🥄🥄🥄 ❧◦·

Once again, I turned to Isabella Beeton's *Book of Household Management* for what to serve for dessert at a Victorian dinner. Eliza Acton, who preceded Beeton (she died in 1859), was another famous cookbook author who provides a recipe that is almost identical to Beeton's. The following recipes are only slightly modified versions of this old-fashioned dessert. To clear up confusion, *pudding* in British English also means "dessert."

APPLE VERSION

2 to 3 tablespoons vegetable oil, for coating the pan

3 pounds sweet apples, such as Gala (about 6)

½ cup sugar plus 2 tablespoons for sprinkling

1 teaspoon ground cinnamon, for sprinkling

1½ cups whole milk, at room temperature

½ cup heavy cream, at room temperature

2 large eggs, at room temperature

1 teaspoon pure vanilla extract

1 cup all-purpose flour

1. Adjust the oven rack to the middle position and preheat the oven to 350°F. Pour enough oil into a 9-inch-by-13-inch pan to coat the bottom. Put the pan into the oven to heat, about 5 minutes. While the pan is heating, peel, core, and slice the apples. (A corer/slicer makes short work of this.)

2. Pull the pan out of the oven and immediately place the apple slices in the hot pan. Gently shake the pan to even out the layer of apples. Mix the sugar and cinnamon in a small bowl and sprinkle the mixture over the apples; then place back in the oven for 20 minutes.

3. While the apples are in the oven, prepare the batter. In a large mixing bowl, whisk together the milk, cream, sugar, eggs, and vanilla until well blended. Add the flour and whisk to combine. When the apples are finished baking, give the batter a final stir with the whisk and pour it over the apples. Bake for 45 minutes, until puffed around the edges and the pudding is set. Remove from the oven and sprinkle generously with more sugar.

4. Serve pudding warm or at room temperature.

Serves 10

Blueberry Version

1 to 2 tablespoons vegetable oil, for
    coating the pan
12 ounces (about 2 cups) fresh or
    frozen blueberries
1 cup whole milk, at room
    temperature

¼ cup heavy cream, at room
    temperature
½ cup sugar
1 teaspoon pure vanilla extract
2 large eggs, at room temperature
1 cup all-purpose flour

1. Adjust the oven rack to the middle position and preheat the oven to 350°F.
    Pour enough oil into the bottom of an 8-inch square pan to coat and put the
    pan in the oven to heat, about 5 minutes. When the pan is hot, pour in the
    blueberries and bake, uncovered, for 15 minutes.

2. While the blueberries are in the oven, whisk together the milk, cream, sugar,
    vanilla, and eggs in a large mixing bowl. Whisk in the flour, whisking vigorously
    to smooth out lumps.

3. When the blueberries are ready, give the batter another whisk and pour it over
    the blueberries. Bake for 30 minutes, until the edges are puffed and the pud-
    ding is set.

4. Serve the pudding warm or at room temperature.

Serves 8

Polly's Dinner with All the Nice Parts Left Out

· Toad in the Hole · Peas and Carrots ·

The Nice Parts

· Sticky Toffee Pudding · Strawberries with Cream ·

Because Polly can't satisfactorily explain to her family her prolonged absence, dirty face, and filthy clothing, she is given dinner "with all the nice parts left out and sent to bed for two solid hours." C. S. Lewis informs us that this punishment "was a thing that happened to one quite often in those days" (*The Magician's Nephew*, chapter 7).

···⊰[TOAD IN THE HOLE]⊱···

A very typical, plain, sensible dinner, just what Polly deserves, this savory pudding is based on the more famous Yorkshire pudding. A Yorkshire pudding type of batter is poured over sausages and then baked. This version offers a combination of herbs to perk up the flavor of the pudding. Why is it called toad in the hole? Nobody knows!

1 pound of your favorite meat or
    vegetarian sausages
2 cups all-purpose flour
½ teaspoon salt
¼ teaspoon ground black pepper
½ teaspoon dried sage

1 tablespoon onion powder
8 tablespoons (½ cup) butter, melted
1½ cups whole milk, at room
    temperature
2 eggs, at room temperature

1.   Adjust the oven rack to the middle position and preheat the oven to 425°F. Spray a 9-inch-by-13-inch pan with baking spray and line up the sausages in the pan.

2. Whisk together the flour, salt, pepper, sage, and onion powder in a large mixing bowl. In a separate mixing bowl, whisk together the milk, butter, and eggs. Pour the milk mixture into the flour mixture and whisk just until combined. The batter will be lumpy.

3. Pour the batter over the sausages. Spread and smooth the batter with a rubber spatula. Bake for 10 minutes. Reduce the temperature to 350°F and bake another 20 minutes, rotating the pan halfway through the baking time, until the pudding is set. It will be a pale color but golden around the edges.

4. Serve warm or at room temperature.

Serves 6 to 8

·⊰[peas and carrots ♪♪♪]⊱·

1 pound frozen mixed peas
and carrots
2 tablespoons butter

Salt, to taste
Freshly ground black pepper, to taste

1. Place the peas and carrots in a medium pot and add just enough water to cover the vegetables. Bring to a boil, then reduce the heat and simmer until crisp-tender, about 5 to 7 minutes. Drain the peas and carrots and return to the pot.

2. Add the butter, salt, and pepper and toss until melted and combined.

Serves 4 to 6

The Nice Parts

·-·] STICKY TOFFEE PUDDING 🥄🥄🥄 [·-·

Though sticky toffee pudding has only been popular since the late twentieth century, there is some evidence that it has been around a lot longer, since at least as early as 1907. Sticky toffee pudding certainly follows the tradition of the great British steamed puddings from the long-ago past, and it happens to be a favorite of the Duchess of Cambridge, Kate Middleton.

PUDDING

1 cup chopped dates

1 cup boiling water

1 teaspoon baking soda

2 cups all-purpose flour

1 teaspoon baking powder

½ teaspoon salt

12 tablespoons (¾ cup) butter, at
  room temperature

1 cup dark brown sugar

2 large eggs, at room temperature

1 teaspoon pure vanilla extract

TOFFEE SAUCE

½ cup heavy cream

½ cup golden syrup or light corn
  syrup

1 teaspoon black treacle or dark
  molasses

1 teaspoon pure vanilla extract

1. To make the pudding, grease and flour a pudding mold and set aside. Place the dates in a bowl. Mix the boiling water and baking soda and pour over the dates. Soak for about 10 minutes, until soft. Process in a blender or food processor until smooth.

2. In a large mixing bowl, whisk together the flour, baking powder, and salt and set aside. In a separate mixing bowl, using an electric mixer, beat the butter and sugar until light and fluffy, scraping down the sides as needed, about 5 minutes. Add the eggs one at a time, beating after each until incorporated. Add the processed date mixture and beat until incorporated. Add

the flour mixture and mix on the slowest speed until combined.

3. Scrape into a pudding mold and seal with the lid. Place a small plate like a saucer upside down in a pot large enough to accommodate the pudding. The upside-down plate will support the pudding mold in the water. Fill the pot with water to come halfway up the sides of the pudding. Bring to a boil, then reduce to a simmer and cook for 3 hours, checking the water level occasionally and topping up with water as needed.

4. Remove the pudding from the pot and make the sauce.

5. To make the sauce, combine the heavy cream, golden syrup or corn syrup, and black treacle or molasses in a medium saucepan over medium heat and cook, stirring constantly. As the mixture comes to a boil, continue cooking and stirring until the mixture thickens enough to coat the back of a spoon, about 10 minutes. The mixture will expand as it cooks. Remove from the heat and stir in the vanilla.

6. Remove the lid from the still-warm pudding and invert onto a large plate. To serve, cut generous slices and pour warm toffee sauce over each serving.

Serves 8

> Although the pudding is traditionally served warm, it is every bit as delicious at room temperature.
>
> This pudding can be baked. Preheat the oven to 350°F. Spray a 9-inch square baking pan with baking spray. Scrape the batter into the pan and smooth the top with a rubber spatula. Bake for 30 to 40 minutes, until the cake feels firm when touched lightly in the center. Cool the cake in the pan and cut into squares. Serve with the toffee sauce. The cake version will be lighter, fluffier, and drier than the dense pudding.

⊷] STRAWBERRIES WITH CREAM 🍴🍴🍴 [⊶

This is quite possibly the oldest and still the best way to serve strawberries as an elegant dessert. The word *strawberry* refers to the "straying" runners of the plant. Runners are stems that help the plants spread or "stray" by putting down new roots. The Vikings believed that the wife of the Norse god Odin, Frigga, carried the spirits of children inside strawberries to the afterlife.

1 pint strawberries, crowns removed, sliced
1 cup heavy cream

¼ cup confectioners' sugar
1 teaspoon pure vanilla extract

1. In a mixing bowl, lightly mash the strawberry slices with a fork. If desired, you can leave the strawberry slices whole.
2. In a separate bowl, whisk together the heavy cream, confectioners' sugar, and vanilla until stiff peaks form.
3. Gently fold the whipped cream into the strawberries and scoop into bowls. Serve immediately.

Serves 4

THE WHITE WITCH'S EXTRAVAGANT LUNCH IN OUR WORLD

· *Julienne Soup* · *Chicken Croquettes* ·

· *Lamb Chops with Mushrooms and Sage* · *Fried Sole Fillets* ·

· *Green Bean Salad with Almond Crunch* ·

· *Grape Jelly with Whipped Cream* ·

· *Custard Sponge Sandwich with Chocolate Glaze* ·

Uncle Andrew is finally angry enough to overcome his dread of the White Witch and tell her off for all her antics, not least of which includes paying for an extravagant lunch whose negative effects he is still feeling. As you have seen, the size and richness of a typical Victorian dinner really could give one indigestion (*The Magician's Nephew*, chapter 9).

ᵉ᷉[JULIENNE SOUP 🥄🥄🥄]ᵉ᷉

Julienne soup is named after the style of cutting the vegetables that go into it. To julienne a vegetable means to cut it into long, thin strips, a rather painstaking task, I must admit, but with very pretty results. A mandoline with a julienne blade will make the job easier.

2 tablespoons vegetable oil
1 onion, cut in half pole to pole and sliced
2 carrots, julienned
2 quarts chicken broth
2 celery ribs, julienned

2 cups frozen peas (keep frozen until ready to use)
1 turnip, julienned (see sidebar)
1 bunch leeks, cleaned very well and julienned (see sidebar)

1 heart romaine lettuce, outer leaves
    peeled away and reserved for
    another use, inner pale leaves
    sliced into strips

Salt, to taste
Freshly ground black pepper, to taste

To get even strips out of the round turnip, thinly slice off the rounded edges. You should now have a rectangle. Slice the rectangle into ⅛-inch-thick slices; then slice each slice in ⅛-inch-wide strips. The leeks are challenging to julienne. First cut them in half lengthwise and wash them well under running water to get rid of the soil. Divide the leeks into layers, slice long, thin strips off of each layer, and then cut those into lengths of 2 inches.

1. Heat the oil in a Dutch oven or large pot. Add the onion, carrots, celery, and turnip and cook over medium-high heat, stirring frequently, until the vegetables are softened and the onions just begin turning brown, about 10 minutes. Add the broth, leeks, lettuce, salt, and pepper and bring to a boil. Reduce to a simmer and cook for another 30 minutes, until the vegetables are tender and the lettuce is wilted.

2. Turn off the heat and add the frozen peas, allowing them to sit in the hot liquid a few minutes to cook through.

Serves 8 to 10

···⊰[CHICKEN CROQUETTES ╱╱╱]⊱···

Croquettes is a French word for delicious, fried little cakes; the word was adopted into the English language in the 1700s. A croquette is usually a mixture of minced poultry (chicken or turkey) or fish bound up with a velouté (a sauce made by thickening broth with a roux, a paste made with fat and flour), coated with eggs and breadcrumbs, and fried. Although today the patty shape is used, early croquettes could have been egg-shaped or even rectangular. Croquettes are not hard to make, but because they involve lots of steps, I awarded the recipe the difficult rating. Because it's time consuming, save this recipe for a special occasion, like a birthday.

2 to 2½ pounds bone-in, skin-on
    chicken breasts (about 2 breasts)
1 carrot, peeled and cut into chunks

1 celery rib, cut into chunks
2 cups chicken broth
1 tablespoon vegetable oil

1 onion, chopped
1 tablespoon all-purpose flour
4 large eggs
¼ teaspoon dried sage
½ teaspoon salt
¼ teaspoon freshly ground black pepper

Vegetable oil, for frying
1 cup seasoned breadcrumbs, or
  breadcrumbs seasoned with salt,
  pepper, and dried parsley, for
  coating

1. Place the chicken, carrot, celery rib, and chicken broth into a medium sauce-pan and bring to a simmer. Simmer for 1 hour, until the chicken and vegeta-bles are tender. Strain through a fine-mesh sieve and cool. Reserve the broth. (You can chill the broth and skim off the fat, or you can use a fat separator to measure out ½ cup of broth.)

2. While the chicken is cooling, heat the oil in a skillet. Add the onion and cook over medium-high heat, stirring frequently, until well browned, about 10 minutes. Sprinkle the flour over the onions and stir to combine. Pour in ½ cup of the reserved broth and stir constantly until smooth. Continue cooking, stirring frequently, until very thick, about 5 minutes.

3. When the chicken and vegetables are cool, remove the chicken from the bones and break into small pieces. Put the chicken, carrot, and celery into a food processor and pulse just until the mixture is crumbly. Transfer the chicken mixture to a large mixing bowl.

4. Add the sauce to the chicken mixture and mix well. Whisk 1 egg with the sage, salt, and pepper; add it to the chicken mixture and mix well. Refrigerate until stiff, about 1 hour.

5. Beat the remaining eggs in a large, shallow bowl. Place the breadcrumbs in another large, shallow bowl. Form the cold chicken mixture into 12 patty shapes. Coat each patty first with the eggs and then with the breadcrumbs.

6. Fill a skillet about a quarter inch up the sides with the oil and turn on the heat to medium-high. When the oil is hot (it should bubble immediately when a small bit of croquette is dropped into it), fry on each side until deep golden brown, about 5 minutes per side. Transfer to a paper towel–lined plate to drain.

Makes about 1 dozen croquettes

·≈[LAMB CHOPS WITH MUSHROOMS AND SAGE ♪♪♪]≈·

Because of its fattiness, lamb is often cooked with an acidic ingredient such as wine or vinegar to cut the fat.

4 shoulder lamb chops
Salt, for sprinkling
Freshly ground black pepper
2 tablespoons vegetable oil
1 medium onion, chopped

5 ounces mushrooms, sliced
½ cup dry red wine
1 cup beef broth
½ teaspoon dried sage

1. Sprinkle the lamb chops evenly with the salt and pepper. Sear in a large skillet over high heat until crusty brown, about 5 minutes per side. Transfer to a large plate.

2. Add the oil to the pan. Add the onions and mushrooms and cook over medium-high heat, scraping up the browned bits with a wooden spoon, until the water evaporates, about 10 minutes. Continue cooking, stirring frequently, until well browned. Add the wine, broth, and sage and bring to a simmer.

3. Add the lamb chops back to the pan along with any accumulated juices and simmer until tender, about 15 minutes. Remove the lamb chops, raise the heat to high, and bring the sauce to a boil. Reduce the sauce until it thickens, about 5 minutes. Adjust the seasonings to taste and pour the sauce over the lamb chops.

Serves 4

·≈[FRIED SOLE FILLETS ♪♪♪]≈·

The Greeks called this fish *solea* because they believed that ocean nymphs could use them as sandals (hence the name "sole"). The sole starts out life with one eye on each side of its head, but as it grows, the left eye migrates to the right side. Talk about roving eyes!

½ cup all-purpose flour
3 eggs
1 cup seasoned breadcrumbs or
    breadcrumbs seasoned with salt,
    pepper, and dried parsley

Vegetable oil, for frying
1½ pounds sole fillets

1. Place the flour in a wide, shallow bowl or plate. Crack the eggs into a wide, shallow bowl and beat well. Place the breadcrumbs in another wide, shallow bowl or plate.

2. Pour oil into a skillet to come a half inch up the sides. Heat the oil over medium-high heat. Dredge the fillets in the flour; then dip into the eggs and coat with the breadcrumbs. Fry the fillets on each side over medium-high heat until golden brown, about 5 minutes per side. Transfer to a paper towel–lined plate. Repeat until all the fillets are cooked.

Serves 4 to 6

᭐[green bean salad WITH ALMOND crunch ♪♪♪]᭐

Mrs. Beeton instructs her readers that the best time to pick green beans is when they're young because if they're allowed to grow too long, they become tough and stringy. This roasted salad makes a nice change from steaming (or boiling, as per Mrs. Beeton's method).

2 pounds green beans, washed and
  trimmed
1 cup halved grape tomatoes
2 shallots, chopped
1 tablespoon olive oil
1 tablespoon honey

2 cloves garlic, minced
1½ teaspoons salt
1 teaspoon ground ginger
¼ teaspoon freshly ground black
  pepper
½ cup toasted slivered almonds

1. Preheat the oven to 450°F. Spray a baking sheet with cooking spray and place the green beans, tomatoes, and shallots on the sheet.

2. Combine the oil, honey, garlic, salt, ginger, and pepper in a bowl and mix well. Rub the mixture into the vegetables with your hands.

3. Roast for 30 minutes, until the green beans are shriveled and the ends are charred.

4. Sprinkle individual servings with the almonds, or place the whole lot in a serving dish and sprinkle the almonds over it.

Serves 6

·⋅ᴈ[GRAPE JELLY WITH WHIPPED CREAM 🥄🥄🥄]ᴈ⋅·

Grape juice played an important role in ancient cookery. The ancients used the sour juice of unripe grapes, called verjuice, the way we use vinegar today, and they reduced sweet grape juice to a syrup by boiling it. They used this to flavor sauces or sweeten dishes. Today we drink fresh grape juice or use it in refreshing desserts like this one.

2 cups white grape juice, divided
1 tablespoon powdered gelatin

Sweetened whipped cream, for serving, about ½ cup

1. Pour ½ cup of the grape juice into a bowl and sprinkle the gelatin on top to soften.
2. Pour the rest of the grape juice into a small saucepan and heat until bubbles start to appear at the edges of the pan, about 5 minutes. Add the softened gelatin and stir until completely dissolved.
3. Pour the hot mixture into 4 small glasses and cool to room temperature; then chill until firm. Dollop whipped cream on top before serving.

Serves 4

·⋅ᴈ[CUSTARD SPONGE SANDWICH CAKE WITH CHOCOLATE GLAZE 🥄🥄🥄]ᴈ⋅·

In the UK, *sandwich cake* refers to layer cake, and custard is so very British that it seems to appear in just about every dessert. This dessert has three components. To simplify, you can use a yellow cake mix or store-bought cake for the layers and instant vanilla pudding for the custard filling.

CAKE

2 cups all-purpose flour
1½ teaspoons baking powder
¼ teaspoon salt
12 tablespoons (¾ cup) butter, at room temperature

1½ cups sugar
2 large eggs, at room temperature
1½ teaspoons pure vanilla extract
½ cup whole milk, at room temperature

Custard

1 cup whole milk	2 tablespoons all-purpose flour
¼ cup sugar	¼ cup heavy cream
2 large egg yolks	1½ teaspoons pure vanilla extract

Chocolate Glaze

½ cup heavy cream
6 ounces bittersweet chocolate, chopped

1. To make the cake, adjust the oven rack to the middle position and preheat the oven to 350°F. Grease two 9-inch round cake pans and line the bottoms with parchment paper.

2. Whisk together the flour, baking powder, and salt. In a separate bowl, using an electric mixer, beat the butter and sugar until light and fluffy, scraping down the sides as needed, about 5 minutes. Add the eggs one a time, beating after each until incorporated. Add the vanilla extract and beat until incorporated. Add half the flour mixture and mix on the slowest speed until combined. Stir in the milk on the slowest speed. Add the remaining flour mixture, again mixing with the electric mixer on the slowest speed until combined.

> There is a wonderful flour product on the market called Wondra, which you can find in the baking aisle of your local grocery store. This flour is treated to produce lump-free gravies and sauces, and I have used it successfully in custards as well.

3. Divide the batter between the prepared pans. Bake 30 minutes, until lightly golden and firm when touched lightly in the center. Cool in the pans.

4. To make the custard, heat the milk and sugar in a small saucepan over medium heat, stirring, until hot and steaming but not boiling. Whisk the egg yolks, flour, and cream in a separate bowl until smooth. Pour about ½ cup of the hot milk mixture into the egg yolk mixture while whisking vigorously. Pour the egg yolk mixture slowly into the saucepan while whisking constantly. Continue to cook over medium heat, stirring constantly, until the mixture is thick and bubbling, about 5 minutes. Cook 5 to 7 more minutes to eliminate the raw flour taste, stirring frequently to prevent scorching. Remove from the heat and stir in the vanilla. Sieve into a bowl, cover the surface with plastic wrap, and chill until set.

5. To make the glaze, heat the cream in a small saucepan until it bubbles around the edges. Put the chocolate in a mixing bowl. Pour the cream over the chocolate and let it stand several minutes, then whisk until smooth. If lumps of chocolate remain, heat briefly in the microwave and then stir until smooth.

6. To assemble the cake, invert one of the baking pans, peel the parchment paper from the cake, and lay it on a plate or round cake platter, top side down. Spread the custard over the cake to within ½ inch of the border. Invert the other baking pan, peel the parchment paper from the cake, and lay it top side up over the custard. Spread the glaze on top of the cake. It may drip down the sides a little, only adding to the appeal.

Serves 16

Arguing with Fledge

· Broiled Lamb Chops · Toffee ·

Fledge, the newly winged horse, can't understand the fuss Polly and Digory are making about having no dinner; there's plenty of fresh grass around, isn't there? Polly has to explain to him that humans can't eat grass, just like horses can't eat mutton chops. The hungry children have no choice but to make do with a bag of toffees that Polly finds in her pocket (*The Magician's Nephew*, chapter 12).

·❧[Broiled Lamb Chops ♪ ♪ ♪]❧·

THANKS TO MY BROTHER, JACK POLATSEK, FOR THIS RECIPE.

Now that lamb is cheap and plentiful, it has pretty much replaced mutton on the market, so we'll have to make do with lamb chops instead of the mutton chops that Fledge can't eat and Polly wishes she could have.

4 garlic cloves, minced
1 teaspoon dried rosemary
1 teaspoon kosher salt

½ teaspoon coarsely ground black
  pepper
6 baby rib lamb chops

1. Set the oven rack to about 5 inches below the broiler and preheat the broiler on high.
2. In a small mixing bowl, combine the garlic, rosemary, salt, and pepper to form a paste. Rub the paste over both sides of each lamb chop. Place the lamb chops on a baking sheet and broil 6 to 8 per minutes per side, until crusty brown.

Serves 3, with 2 small ribs per person

··◦[TOFFEE *♪♪♪*]◦··

Toffee is a smooth, hard, crunchy candy made by boiling sugar with butter and cream. To prevent the sugar from recrystallizing, you must add an invert sugar like the corn syrup in this recipe (honey or golden syrup make fine substitutes) and an acid like lemon juice or cream of tartar.

2 cups sugar
⅔ cup whole milk
⅔ cup heavy cream
4 tablespoons (¼ cup) butter
¾ cup light corn syrup

¼ teaspoon salt
¼ teaspoon cream of tartar
1 teaspoon soy lecithin (see sidebar)
1 teaspoon vanilla

1. Grease an 8-inch square pan and line with parchment paper, allowing the paper to come up two of the sides for easy removal. Greasing the bottom and sides helps the paper stick to the pan. Set aside until needed.

2. Combine the sugar, milk, heavy cream, butter, corn syrup, salt, cream of tartar, and soy lecithin in a large saucepan. Cook, stirring constantly, until the sugar is dissolved and the mixture comes to a boil. Wash down the sides of the pan with a pastry brush dipped in hot water. Clip a candy thermometer to the side of the pan and cook over medium-high heat, stirring constantly, until the temperature reaches 280°F.

You can find liquid soy lecithin in health food stores, but you can also leave it out if you don't want the bother. The lecithin emulsifies the fat in the candy mixture, keeping it well mixed with the other ingredients, but you can make fine toffee without it.

3. Remove the pan from the heat and add the vanilla. Stir to combine and pour into the prepared pan. Cool the candy somewhat until it's still warm and soft. Score with a sharp, oiled knife, making 7 cuts in each direction to make 1-inch squares. When the toffee is completely cool, break along the scores. Wrap the candy in squares of parchment or waxed paper to keep them from sticking together.

Makes 64 pieces

Dinner with the Beavers

· Fried Trout ·Boiled Potatoes with Butter ·

· Homemade White Sandwich Bread ·

· Gloriously Sticky Marmalade Roll · Tea ·

No tea with Tumnus for the Pevensies, after all; he's been captured by the White Witch. While the children try to decide what to do, a talking beaver discovers them and invites them into his home for dinner (*The Lion, the Witch and the Wardrobe*, chapter 7).

·≈[Fried Trout 🥄🥄🥄]≈·

According to *The Oxford Companion to Food*, the popularity of trout has caused it to be widely introduced throughout most of the world, so that "trout of one kind or another are now found in every continent except Antarctica." You shouldn't have trouble finding any for this recipe!

½ cup all-purpose flour

3 eggs

1 cup seasoned breadcrumbs, or
breadcrumbs seasoned with salt,
pepper, and dried parsley

Vegetable oil, for frying

1½ pounds trout fillets

1. Place the flour in a wide, shallow bowl or plate. Crack eggs into a wide, shallow bowl and beat well. Place the breadcrumbs in another wide, shallow bowl or plate.

2. Pour oil into a large skillet to come a half inch up the sides. Heat the oil over medium-high heat. Dredge the fillets in the flour, then dip into the eggs and coat with the breadcrumbs. Fry the fillets on each side over medium-high heat until golden brown, about 5 minutes per side. Transfer to a paper towel–lined plate and repeat until all the fillets are cooked.

Serves 4 to 6

·❧ BOILED POTATOES WITH BUTTER ♪♪♪ ❧·

Can you imagine life without potatoes? It seems as if potatoes have always been around, but they arrived fairly late on the scene in Europe. The Spanish explorers first brought this vegetable back to Europe from South America in the sixteenth century, where botanists culti-vated it as a curiosity. Europeans only started eating potatoes in the 1700s, and it took a lot of persuading to get the French and English to just try it.

*2 pounds red-skin potatoes (about 6),
    scrubbed, unpeeled*
3 tablespoons butter

Salt, to taste
Freshly ground black pepper, to taste

1. Cut the potatoes into eighths. Put them in a pot and fill with water to cover. Bring to a boil. Cover, reduce the heat, and simmer until the potatoes are easily pierced with a fork, 20 to 25 minutes.

2. Drain the potatoes and return them to the pot. Add the butter, salt, and pepper and toss until melted and combined.

Serves 4 to 6

·❧ HOMEMADE WHITE SANDWICH BREAD ♪♪♪ ❧·

While the boys are helping Mr. Beaver catch fresh fish for dinner, the girls join Mrs. Beaver in preparing the rest of the meal, including slic-ing the bread (*The Lion, the Witch and the Wardrobe,* chapter 7). Enjoy this delicious bread thickly sliced and slathered with gobs of butter.

4 tablespoons (¼ cup) butter
1 cup whole milk
3 cups all-purpose flour

1 tablespoon (1 packet) instant yeast
1 teaspoon salt

1. Heat the butter and milk in a small saucepan until the butter melts. Keep warm, but don't use the mixture when hot, or it will kill the yeast.

2. In a mixing bowl, whisk together the flour, yeast, and salt. Add the milk mixture

and knead with an electric stand mixer fitted with the dough hook or by hand for 10 minutes, until smooth and elastic.

3. Place the dough in an oiled bowl, turning to coat the dough. Cover with plastic wrap and leave in a warm, draft-free place until doubled in size, 1½ to 2 hours.

4. Spray a loaf pan with baking spray and set aside. Turn the dough out onto a lightly floured work surface, shape it into a loaf, and place it into the prepared loaf pan. Leave to rise until doubled in size, 1½ to 2 hours.

5. Adjust the oven rack to the middle position and preheat the oven to 350°F. Bake the bread for 30 minutes, rotating the pan halfway through baking, until the bread is a pale golden color.

Makes 1 loaf

·ᢀ[GLORIOUSLY STICKY Marmalade ROLL ♪♪♪]ᢀ·

After dinner, Mrs. Beaver pulls a surprise out of the oven: a gloriously sticky marmalade roll. Like jam roly poly and other sticky puddings, this classic was a childhood favorite of many an English boy and girl. Enjoy it, as the Beavers and Pevensies did, with mugs of steaming hot tea.

2 cups all-purpose flour	*½ cup milk, at room temperature*
¼ cup sugar	*1 cup orange marmalade*
¼ teaspoon salt	*1 egg, beaten with 1 tablespoon*
1 tablespoon (1 packet) instant yeast	*water*
4 tablespoons (¼ cup) butter, softened	*1 tablespoon sugar mixed with ½*
2 large egg yolks, at room	*teaspoon ground cinnamon*
temperature	

1. Whisk together the flour, sugar, salt, and yeast. Add the butter, egg yolks, and milk and combine. Knead with an electric stand mixer fitted with the dough hook or by hand for 10 minutes, until the dough is smooth and elastic and comes away cleanly from the sides of the bowl. Place in an oiled bowl, turning to coat the dough. Cover with plastic wrap and let rise in a warm, draft-free place until doubled in size, 1½ to 2 hours.

2. Preheat the oven to 350°F and line a baking sheet with parchment paper.

Roll out the dough on a floured work surface about ¼-inch thick into a rect-angle. Transfer the dough rectangle to the baking sheet (once filled, it will be difficult to move). Spread the marmalade down the center of the rectangle, leaving a 2-inch border on each side. Cut 2-inch-long slits 1 inch apart along the length of the rectangle on both sides. Fold the flaps over the filling. Brush the top of the roll with the beaten egg and sprinkle with the cinnamon sugar.

3.   Bake for 30 minutes, rotating halfway through baking, until golden and bubbling.

Makes 1 roll

CHRISTMAS DINNER FROM FATHER CHRISTMAS

· Roast Goose with Fall Fruit Stuffing ·Easy Cranberry Sauce ·
· Mashed Potatoes with Onion Gravy · Plum Pudding · Christmas Biscuits ·

It is unfortunate for some creatures of Narnia that the White Witch should stumble upon them while they are enjoying a Christmas dinner given to them by Father Christmas. Ignoring Edmund's plea on their behalf, she turns them all to stone, then strikes Edmund viciously for daring to intercede for the traitors (*The Lion, the Witch and the Wardrobe*, chapter 11).

ROAST GOOSE WITH FALL FRUIT STUFFING

THANKS TO CHEF CHRIS KOCH FOR THIS RECIPE.

Roast goose on Christmas is so classic, the Cratchits have it for Christmas dinner in Charles Dickens's famous story *A Christmas Carol*, where they enjoy it with a sage and onion stuffing. Geese have been much prized throughout history, and not just for their succulent flesh or for producing the delicacy known as foie gras: their feathers have been used to make arrows and featherbeds, their quills were used for pens, and their fat has been used for cooking.

4 cups chicken stock
½ cup dried cherries
⅓ cup diced dried apricot halves
⅓ cup diced dried apples
2 tablespoons dried currants (see note about currants on page 42)
3 tablespoons butter
½ cup fresh breadcrumbs

½ cup diced shallot
1 teaspoon fresh thyme
1 teaspoon fresh sage
1 (9- to 12-pound) goose
1 cup water
1 cup white wine
½ cup apricot preserves

1. Bring the stock to a boil. Add the dried fruits, remove from the heat, and steep for 20 minutes. Strain and press the fruit to remove the excess liquid. Set aside and reserve the liquid.

2. In a medium sauté pan, melt the butter. Add the breadcrumbs, shallot, and herbs and stir to combine. Add the breadcrumb mixture to the fruit and stir again. Add enough of the reserved cooking liquid to make a moist stuffing.

3. Preheat the oven to 400°F. Rinse the goose inside and outside. Fill the cavity with the stuffing mixture. Tie the legs together with a piece of kitchen twine and place in a shallow roasting pan. Tuck any excess neck skin under the bird.

4. Roast the goose for 18 to 20 minutes per pound or to an internal temperature of 165°F. Remove the goose from the pan and keep warm. Drain the excess fat from the roasting pan and reserve for other uses. Place the roasting pan on a burner over medium-high heat. Add the water and wine. Bring to a boil and scrape up any browned bits on the bottom of the pan. Stir in the apricot preserves and heat through.

5. Carve the goose and remove the stuffing from the cavity. Serve the goose and stuffing with the apricot sauce.

Serves 6

·≋⟨ Mashed Potatoes with Onion Gravy ⟩≋·

Also featured in the Cratchits' meal in *A Christmas Carol*, mashed potatoes are classic served alongside the main dish at Christmas dinner.

MASHED POTATOES

2 pounds large russet or baking potatoes (about 6), peeled and cut into eighths
½ cup whole milk

4 tablespoons (¼ cup) butter
Salt, to taste
Freshly ground black pepper, to taste

ONION GRAVY

3 tablespoons vegetable oil
1 onion, chopped
2 tablespoons all-purpose flour

2 cups beef broth
Salt, to taste
Freshly ground black pepper, to taste

1. To make the potatoes, place the potatoes in a large pot, cover with water, and bring to a boil. Reduce to a simmer and cook, covered, until easily pierced with a fork, about 25 minutes. Drain the potatoes and return to the pot.

2. Add the milk, butter, salt, and pepper and mash it all together with a potato masher.

3. To make the gravy, heat the oil in a small saucepan. Add the onion and cook until browned. Add the flour and stir to combine. Pour in the beef broth and stir until combined. Bring the mixture to a boil, stirring constantly. Cook over medium heat for another 5 minutes, until the raw flour taste disappears. Taste and season with the salt and pepper.

4. Serve heaps of mashed potatoes drenched in gravy.

Serves 4 to 6

·⋅ PLUM PUDDING ♩♩♪♩]ⓒ··

Plum used to also refer to any dried fruit, especially raisins. This usage still survives in the name of this ancient dish. I sometimes wonder whether Little Jack Horner in the old nursery rhyme pulled out a raisin, rather than the fresh plum that is so often pictured in nursery rhyme books. The plum pudding was the most obvious bit of food Edmund could see the poor Narnian creatures eating before they are turned to stone.

1 cup fresh breadcrumbs (from about
   4 slices bread, crusts removed)
1 cup all-purpose flour
½ cup ground walnuts
1 teaspoon ground cinnamon
½ teaspoon ground ginger
¼ teaspoon ground cloves
¼ teaspoon salt
½ cup raisins
½ cup golden raisins
½ cup chopped almonds

1 cup light or dark brown sugar
12 tablespoons (¾ cup) butter, at
   room temperature
½ cup currants or dried sweetened
   cranberries (see note about
   currants on page 42)
Grated zest of 1 lemon
Grated zest of 1 orange
2 eggs, at room temperature
½ cup orange marmalade
¼ cup brandy

1. Grease a 2-quart pudding mold (see sidebar). Fill a large pot with water. Put a small plate, such as a saucer, upside down on the bottom of the pot, or put a steamer in the pot if you have one. The plate or steamer will support the pudding mold in the water.

2. Whisk together the breadcrumbs, flour, ground walnuts, spices, and salt. In a separate bowl, combine the dried fruits and chopped almonds.

> You can order a good pudding mold with a tight-fitting lid online, but if you want to improvise, any bowl of the same size with a tight-fitting lid (such as Pyrex) will do. The lid may get ruined by the first use, however, so if you're not willing to sacrifice a good lid, simply cover with aluminum foil. Seal it as tightly as you can with rubber bands to prevent steam or water from seeping in.

3. In a large mixing bowl, using an electric mixer, beat the butter with the sugar, lemon zest, and orange zest until light and fluffy, scraping down the sides as needed, about 5 minutes. Add the eggs one at a time, beating after each until incorporated. Add the marmalade and brandy and beat until combined. Add the flour mixture, mixing on the slowest speed until combined. Stir in the dried fruit mixture. Scrape the batter into the mold and snap the cover into place.

4. Place the pudding mold in the pot on top of the overturned saucer. Make sure there is enough water to come halfway up the sides of the mold. Cover the pot, bring to a boil, then reduce the heat and simmer for 3 hours. Check periodically to make sure the pot isn't boiling dry, and top up with water if necessary.

5. Remove the pot from the heat and allow the water to cool slightly before removing the pudding. When the pudding is cool, unmold onto a piece of heavy-duty aluminum foil. Wrap well in the foil and seal in a plastic bag. Store until ready to use, up to 3 months.

6. Before serving, the pudding needs to be reboiled for 3 hours, so make sure to give yourself plenty of time. Replace the pudding into the mold and follow the instructions for boiling. The pudding is supposed to be served warm, so unmold the pudding while it's still warm. Take care! The warm pudding can fall apart easily. Make sure to let the pudding cool down a bit so it's warm, but not hot, when you unmold it. Serve with warm custard sauce (see the custard sauce recipe from the "High Tea after Battle" menu on page 57).

Serves 8

❧ CHRISTMAS BISCUITS 🥄🥄🥄 ❧

Nuts and warm spices...nothing says Christmas more than these holiday cookies.

2 cups all-purpose flour

1 cup ground walnuts

¾ teaspoon baking soda

½ teaspoon salt

1½ teaspoons ground cinnamon

½ teaspoon ground nutmeg

¼ teaspoon ground allspice

¼ teaspoon ground cloves

16 tablespoons (1 cup) butter, at
    room temperature

1 cup sugar

2 eggs, at room temperature

1. Adjust the oven racks to the upper and lower middle positions. Preheat the oven to 350°F. Line 2 baking sheets with parchment paper. Whisk the flour, ground walnuts, baking soda, salt, and spices in a large mixing bowl.

2. In a separate bowl, beat the butter and sugar with an electric mixer until light and fluffy, scraping down the sides as needed, about 5 minutes. Add the eggs one at a time, beating after each until incorporated. Add the flour mixture and mix on the slowest speed until combined.

3. Divide the dough in half, wrap in plastic wrap, and chill for at least 1 hour. If the dough is too hard to roll out, leave it out at room temperature until it softens. Working with one piece of dough at a time, place the dough on a floured work surface and sprinkle the top with more flour to prevent sticking. Roll the dough ¼-inch thick and stamp out rounds of dough with a 2-inch cookie cutter. Lay the cookies ½ inch apart on the cookie sheets.

4. Bake for 10 minutes, rotating and switching the pans halfway through the baking time. The cookies will be pale but should look dry.

Makes about 6½ dozen

Shasta's Dinner as Corin

· *Boiled Lobster* · *Chickpea Salad* · *Snipe Stuffed with Almonds and Truffles* ·

· *Chicken Livers with Rice Pilaf* · *Gooseberry Fool* · *Mulberry Fool* ·

· *Refreshing Mango Sorbet* · *Melons* ·

· *Ginger Beer, White Grape Juice, or White Wine* ·

Shasta is at a loss. The Narnians still think he's Prince Corin, and when they find out he isn't—as they surely will eventually—what will they do to him? He has heard all their plans. Will they kill him? While he's agonizing over his predicament, Tumnus the Faun brings him a lavish dinner (*The Horse and His Boy*, chapter 5).

·≈] BOILED LOBSTER [≈·

THANKS TO CHEF CHRIS KOCH FOR THIS RECIPE.

Adult lobsters can defend themselves so well that pretty much their only predator is man. They can spot danger easily with their eye stalks, and then they can move away very fast. They are also covered with formidable armor!

2 (1½ pound) lobsters, live	4 lemon wedges
4 gallons boiling salted water	2 ounces butter, melted

1. Drop the lobsters into the boiling water. Bring the water back to a boil, reduce to a simmer, and cook the lobsters until done, approximately 12 minutes.
2. Remove the lobsters from the pot, drain, and serve immediately with lemon wedges and melted butter on the side.
3. If you prefer to eat the lobsters cold, drop them in a sink of ice water to stop the cooking process. When cool enough to handle, remove the meat from the shell following the procedures discussed in the "Dinner in Those Days" menu on page 91.

Serves 2

·⦙ CHICKPEA SALAD 🥄🥄🥄 ⦙·

Tumnus the Faun serves Shasta salads, so I chose a classic Mediterranean version to reflect the Mediterranean-ness of the Calormenes. In Middle Eastern countries, chickpeas are most famously used to make hummus or falafel, but they are tossed into salads and cooked into soups as well. In the Balkans and the Middle East, street vendors sell them roasted and salted or sweetened.

*1½ cups dried chickpeas, cooked (see
    sidebar), or 2 (15-ounce) cans,
    rinsed and drained*
1 cucumber, peeled and chopped
1 cup grape tomatoes, halved
1 green pepper, chopped
½ red onion, chopped

¼ cup olive oil
Juice of 1 lemon
2 garlic cloves, minced
1 teaspoon salt
½ teaspoon ground cumin
½ teaspoon ground coriander
¼ teaspoon ground cayenne pepper

1. Place the chickpeas, cucumber, grape tomatoes, green pepper, and onion in a large mixing bowl.

2. In a separate bowl, combine the olive oil, lemon juice, garlic, salt, cumin, coriander, and cayenne pepper. Whisk until emulsified, pour over the salad, and toss to combine.

3. Serve immediately, or chill and serve within 3 days. Toss again before serving.

> To cook the dried chickpeas, soak them in water overnight. Drain them, put them in a pot, and cover with water. Bring to a simmer and cook, covered, for 1½ to 2 hours, until tender.

Serves 8

·⦙ SNIPE STUFFED WITH ALMONDS AND TRUFFLES 🥄🥄🥄 ⦙·

THANKS TO CHEF CHRIS KOCH FOR THIS RECIPE.

The snipe is a tiny bird whose long bill makes up most of its size, which is why this recipe advises two birds per serving. Because they're not easy to find, you can substitute quail or dove. Truffles are also not easy to find; they're an expensive delicacy and always have been. Humans have a hard time finding them because the edible parts grow underground, so pigs and dogs are used to snuffle out the truffles. Pigs are a problem, though; being pigs, once they find the truffles, they want them all to themselves. Plutarch, the first-century Greek historian, believed that lightning was necessary for the creation of truffles.

8 snipe (you can substitute any small game bird, such as quail or dove), cleaned

4 tablespoons butter

½ cup finely chopped yellow onion

2 cups breadcrumbs

2 ounces minced fresh or preserved black truffles

¼ cup crushed blanched almonds

½ teaspoon kosher salt

¼ teaspoon freshly ground black pepper

1 cup chicken broth

1. Rinse the snipe and pat dry. Preheat the oven to 325°F. In a skillet, melt the butter over medium-high heat. Add the onions and cook, stirring, until tender, about 5 minutes. Add the breadcrumbs and stir to combine well. Cook, stirring frequently, for 3 minutes or until lightly browned. Add the truffles, almonds, salt, and pepper and stir to combine. Stir in the broth and remove from the heat. Let cool slightly.

2. Fill the cavities of each bird with the breadcrumb mixture, and tie the legs together with a small piece of cotton string. Place on a rack in a shallow roasting pan. Roast for 30 to 35 minutes, to an internal temperature of 165°F.

Serves 4

·⊰ CHICKEN LIVERS WITH RICE PILAF ⧸⧸⧸ ⊱·

The liver of some animals is considered a delicacy, such as the specially fattened goose liver known as foie gras. But of all fowl, chicken liver is the most commonly eaten.

CHICKEN LIVERS

2 tablespoons oil

1 onion, chopped

1 pound chicken livers

Rice

2 tablespoons olive oil

1½ cups long-grain white rice

3 cups chicken broth

½ cup toasted pine nuts (see sidebar)

¼ cup golden raisins, optional

½ teaspoon ground cardamom

Salt, to taste

1. To make the chicken livers, heat the oil in a large skillet. Add the onion and cook over high heat, stirring frequently, until browned, about 7 minutes. Add the chicken livers and reduce the heat to medium-high. Continue to cook until the livers reach an internal temperature of 165°F and are uniformly brown with a firm texture.

2. To make the rice, heat the oil in a medium saucepan. Add the rice and cook over medium heat, stirring constantly, until the rice is well coated and aromatic. Add the broth and bring to a boil. Immediately reduce the heat to the lowest setting so the rice is barely simmering and cook until the broth is absorbed and the rice is tender, 20 to 25 minutes.

3. Add the olive oil, pine nuts, raisins, if using, and cardamom to the pot. Toss to combine. Taste and adjust the seasoning with salt. Keep covered until ready to serve. Fluff with a fork before serving.

4. Serve the chicken livers with the rice on the side.

Serves 4

> To toast the pine nuts, spread them on a baking sheet and toast at 350°F for no more than 5 minutes, as the nuts burn easily.

·∘⟦ GOOSEBERRY FOOL 🥄🥄🥄 ⟧∘·

A fool is an old-fashioned British dessert made by mashing fruit (the name comes from the French world *fouler*, which means "to mash") and mixing it with cream. Before forks came into popular use in Great Britain in the 1700s, the cream was simply mixed into the fruit. Later, the cream was also whipped. As for gooseberries, it's assumed that they are so named because the British may have used them in a sauce that was eaten with goose. To top and tail gooseberries means to remove the stem and blossom ends.

12 ounces red or green fresh
gooseberries, topped and tailed,
or 1 (15-ounce) can green
gooseberries in light syrup

¾ cup granulated sugar
1¼ cups heavy cream
¼ cup confectioners' sugar

1. If using fresh gooseberries, cook the gooseberries with the granulated sugar until soft. Push through a sieve using a rubber spatula, pressing down to extract as much juice as possible. Discard the pulp and reserve the juice. Cool the mixture to room temperature and chill. If using canned gooseberries, drain the gooseberries and sieve them in the same way. Then stir in the sugar.

2. Whip the heavy cream with the confectioners' sugar in a large mixing bowl until stiff peaks form. Fold in the chilled gooseberry mixture, leaving the mixture marbled. Spoon into 4 glasses or bowls and serve immediately.

Serves 4

> Fresh gooseberries are almost impossible to find. I lucked out and found the red ones in mid-July at the local supermarket. Canned gooseberries are not all that easy to find, either, but you can order them by the case on the Internet.

ᓚ MULBERRY FOOL ᓗ

Mulberry trees, which are so old they are even mentioned in the Bible, were introduced into Britain by the Romans. A certain species of mulberry trees provides the leaves that silkworms need to produce their silk. In an attempt to produce their own silk at around the turn of the seventeenth century, the royal family imported the wrong type of mulberry trees, which they then tried to get their silkworms to feed on. Needless to say, the project failed.

Because mulberries are not sold commercially, this recipe substitutes blackberries.

*12 ounces fresh or frozen
    blackberries, thawed if frozen
½ cup granulated sugar*

*1¼ cups heavy cream
¼ cup confectioners' sugar*

1. Push the blackberries through a sieve using a rubber spatula, pressing down to extract as much juice as possible. Discard the pulp. Stir in the sugar.

2. Whip the heavy cream with the confectioners' sugar in a large mixing bowl until stiff peaks form. Fold in the blackberry mixture, leaving the mixture marbled. Spoon into 6 glasses or bowls and serve immediately.

Serves 6

REFRESHING MANGO SORBET 🥄🥄🥄

Mangos grow well in hot climates, like Calormen's. This recipe uses frozen mango to save the expense of buying fresh mangoes, as well as the tedium of peeling and chopping them. You will need an ice cream maker for this recipe.

2 (12-ounce) packages frozen mango,
    thawed
1¼ cups sugar

Juice of 1 lemon
¾ cup water

1. Place the mango, sugar, lemon juice, and water in the bowl of a food processor. Process until smooth, 1 or 2 minutes.
2. Push the mixture through a sieve with a rubber spatula, stirring and pressing to extract as much juice as possible. Discard the pulp. Chill until cold.
3. Freeze in an ice cream maker according to the manufacturer's instructions. Transfer to an airtight container and freeze until firm.
4. Allow the sorbet to soften at room temperature for 15 minutes before serving.

Makes about 4 cups

MELONS

For dessert, include a platter of cut-up melons.

GINGER BEER, WHITE GRAPE JUICE, OR WHITE WINE

Serve ginger beer (see the recipe from the "The Sweets They Had in Those Days" menu on page 41) and white grape juice, or white wine for the adults.

LUNCH WITH LUNE

· *Cold Sliced Chicken Breast* · *Game Pie* ·

· *Ginger Beer or Wine, Bread, and Cheese* ·

Shasta, who has discovered he is actually of royal blood and that his name is really Cor, enjoys lunch with the plainly dressed King Lune of Archenland after Aravis goes off with Lucy, talking girl stuff (*The Horse and His Boy*, chapter 15).

COLD SLICED CHICKEN BREAST

The lunch that Shasta has consists of cold poultry, so we're at liberty to choose which type. Chicken, because of its cheapness and ubiquity, is the obvious choice.

2 tablespoons olive oil
½ teaspoon dried sage
½ teaspoon dried marjoram
½ teaspoon dried tarragon

½ teaspoon salt
¼ teaspoon freshly ground black
 pepper
2 chicken breasts, bone-in, skin-on

1. Preheat the oven to 450°F. Combine the oil, herbs, salt, and pepper and rub the mixture over the chicken. Place the chicken in a small pan (such as an 8-inch square pan) and bake, uncovered, until a thermometer inserted into the thickest part of the breast reads 165°F, about 30 minutes.

2. Remove from the oven and cool before slicing. Carefully cut away the breast meat from the bone and slice into uniform slices. Serve at room temperature or chilled.

Serves 4

·:](Game Pie ⫝ ⫝ ⫝)[:·

THIS RECIPE IS THANKS TO CHEF CHRIS KOCH, WHO MADE IT WITH HIS CLASS AT DREXEL UNIVERSITY FOR A HUNTER'S DINNER.

Game refers to animals (and even fish) that are hunted rather than domesticated, although deer and pigeons, which are farm raised, are still considered game.

PIE DOUGH

2½ cups all-purpose flour

½ teaspoon salt

8 ounces lard, chilled and cubed

½ to ¾ cup ice water, as needed

FILLING

1 (2- to 3-pound) pheasant, cleaned and dressed

1 (2- to 2 ½–pound) rabbit, cleaned and dressed and cut into pieces

Salt, for seasoning

Pepper, for seasoning

½ pound bacon

2 cups chopped yellow onion

1 pound venison shoulder, cut into ½-inch cubes

1 cup port wine

3 tablespoons all-purpose flour

3 cups beef or chicken stock

10 ounces wild mushrooms, cut into bite-size pieces

2 cloves garlic, minced

1 tablespoon Worcestershire sauce

1 egg, beaten

ASPIC (BROTH SET WITH GELATIN)

4 allspice berries

2 pinches ground nutmeg

6 whole black peppercorns

1 teaspoon dried thyme

2 bay leaves

1 carrot, chopped

1 medium onion, chopped

2 cups consommé (clear chicken, beef, or game stock, or store-bought chicken or beef broth)

4 whole cloves

0.4-ounce package gelatin

I. To make the dough in a food processor, place the flour and salt in a food processor. Add the lard. Pulse until the mixture resembles coarse meal, with larger pieces of fat remaining. Add ½ cup water and pulse until the dough begins to come together in a ball. If the dough is too dry, add the remaining water 1 tablespoon at a time.

2. To make the dough by hand, place the flour and salt in a bowl. Using a pastry knife, cut the lard into the flour until pea-sized pieces are formed. Add ½ cup water and mix with a rubber spatula until the dough begins to clump together. If the dough is too dry, add the remaining water 1 tablespoon at a time.

3. Divide the dough in half and form into disks. Wrap in plastic wrap and refrigerate until needed, up to 3 days.

4. Preheat the oven to 400°F. Season the pheasant inside and out with salt and pepper. Place the pheasant breast side up on a rack in a large roasting pan. Roast for 30 minutes. Reduce the temperature to 325°F and roast 20 to 22 minutes per pound, or until the juices run clear when pierced with a fork at the thickest part of the thigh. Remove from the pan and cool.

5. While the pheasant roasts, cook the rabbit. Place the rabbit into a large casserole or Dutch oven. Add enough water to barely cover the bottom of the casserole. Season the rabbit with salt and pepper. Cover and cook over medium heat, turning the pieces often, until tender, about 1 hour. Add small amounts of water if necessary to prevent scorching. Remove the rabbit from the casserole and cool.

6. While the pheasant and rabbit are cooking, prepare the venison. In a large skillet, cook the bacon until crispy. Remove the bacon and drain on paper towels, then chop finely. Leave the fat in the skillet. Heat the skillet with the fat over medium-high heat. Add the chopped onions and cook, stirring, until lightly browned, about 10 minutes. Season the venison with salt and pepper. Add the venison and cook, stirring often, until the cubes are lightly browned on all sides, about 5 minutes.

7. Remove the skillet from the stovetop and add the port. Return the skillet to the heat. Cook, stirring to scrape up any browned bits on the bottom of the pan, until the port has reduced by half, about 5 minutes. Stir in the flour, smoothing the lumps as you stir, and pour in the stock. Reduce the heat to medium-low, cover, and simmer for 40 minutes. Add the mushrooms and stir. Continue cooking another 20 minutes, until the venison is very tender.

8. Remove the skin, bones, and gristle from the pheasant and rabbit. Cut the

pheasant and rabbit into bite-size pieces and add to the skillet with the venison. Stir in the garlic and Worcestershire sauce. Adjust the seasoning with salt and pepper. Remove from the heat and cool completely.

9. Set the oven rack to the middle position and preheat the oven to 375°F. Remove the dough from the refrigerator. On a floured work surface, roll one disk large enough to line a 9-inch deep-dish pie plate with a ¾-inch overhang. Roll the other disk large enough to cover the top of the pie plate with a ¾-inch overlap.

10. Line the pie plate with the dough, spoon in the meat filling, and pour any liquid in the skillet over the filling. Top with the second dough circle. Press the overhanging dough together and roll up to create a ring around the top edge of the pie plate. Press down lightly with the tines of a fork or create another decorative pattern. Using a sharp knife, cut a hole in the center of the top about ½ inch in diameter. Brush the top of the dough with the beaten egg.

11. Place the pie on a rimmed baking sheet and put it in the oven. Immediately reduce the temperature to 350°F and bake for 30 to 40 minutes, or until the crust is golden brown. Remove the pie from the oven and cool completely.

12. While the pie cools, prepare the aspic. Place all the ingredients except the gelatin in a medium saucepan. Bring to a simmer and let simmer for 20 minutes. Strain out the solids and discard, and return the liquid to the pan off the heat. Whisk in the gelatin and dissolve completely. Cool to room temperature. As the liquid cools, it will begin to firm up. Make sure it doesn't get thicker than a syrupy consistency. Carefully pour the aspic into the hole on top of the pie (a funnel is handy to use), and chill completely or overnight. Slice the pie into wedges.

Serves 8

⊰[GINGER BEER OR WINE, BREAD, AND CHEESE]⊱

Serve this meal as Shasta/Cor had it, with wine for the adults and ginger beer for the kids (see the recipe from the "The Sweets They Had in Those Days" menu on page 41), plus bread and cheese. For freshly baked bread, you can use any of the bread recipes in this book.

Prince Caspian with His Subjects

· *Oaten Meal Cakes* · *Apples, Herbs, Wine, and Cheese* ·

The Old Narnians that Prince Caspian stumbles upon in his flight from his murderous uncle are now taking him around to meet his subjects. The centaur Glenstorm broaches the subject of war, then the centaurs provide lunch (*Prince Caspian*, chapter 6).

⇥ Oaten Meal Cakes ♪♪♪ ⇤

Oats have been a major staple in Scotland for centuries because of their hardiness in cold climates. Samuel Johnson, the great eighteenth-century lexicographer, wrote sneeringly in his famous *Dictionary of the English Language* that oats are "a grain, which in England is generally given to horses, but in Scotland supports the people." (He later confessed that he meant this as an insult.) Soldiers on the march in the 1300s would take bags of oats with them, and when they would stop for meals, they would moisten the oats with water and cook the small cakes over a fire.

I tried making oaten meal cakes in their simplest version, but they were very crumbly. Oats are low in gluten, which is what gives dough its structure, so I fixed the problem with just a half cup of whole-wheat flour, which is high in gluten. This lightly sweetened version of these dense cakes makes a great breakfast that can be eaten on the run and that will keep hunger at bay for hours.

3 cups old-fashioned rolled oats
¼ cup buttermilk
4 tablespoons butter, melted
1 large egg, at room temperature

⅓ cup dark brown sugar
½ teaspoon salt
½ cup white whole-wheat flour
  (see sidebar)

1. Adjust the oven racks to the upper and lower middle positions and preheat the oven to 350°F. Line 2 baking sheets with parchment paper and set aside.

2. Place 2 cups of the oats in a bowl and stir in the buttermilk. Cover and let the mixture sit a few hours or overnight. For a smoother texture, process just the oats in a food processor until finely ground.

3. In a small mixing bowl, whisk together the butter, egg, sugar, and salt until combined. Pour this mixture onto the oat mixture and work it in with a wooden spoon. Add the flour and mix well. Stir in the remaining cup of oats. Using a spring-loaded ice cream scoop, portion out the dough onto the baking sheets, forming 12 cakes, or divide the dough into 12 portions if you don't have an ice cream scoop. Flatten the cakes with the heel of your palm.

> You can find white whole-wheat flour in the baking aisle of your supermarket. The only brand I've ever seen is King Arthur. I like to use the white whole-wheat flour for its lighter color and texture.

4. Bake for 12 to 14 minutes, switching and rotating the pans halfway through baking, until the cakes are firm. Eat plain, or serve warm with butter and jam.

Makes 1 dozen cakes

⋅⊰[Apples, Herbs, Wine, and Cheese]⊱⋅

Wine (or grape juice for the kids), cheese, and apples will make a nice accompaniment for the oaten meal cakes. Although C. S. Lewis mentions herbs as an accompaniment, I recommend foregoing them.

SUPPER WITH TRUMPKIN THE DWARF

· Apple-Stuffed "Bear" Steaks (Stuffed Sandwich Steaks) ·

Tramping around with Trumpkin the Dwarf has its benefits. First, he saves the Pevensies' lives by shooting a bear that is about to attack them; then he shows them how to roast the bear steaks with apples to make a mouthwatering meal. For our purposes, sandwich steaks will have to stand in for the bear (*Prince Caspian*, chapter 10).

⋯⊰[APPLE-STUFFED "BEAR" STEAKS (STUFFED SANDWICH STEAKS) 🥄🥄🥄]⊱⋯

1 to 1½ pounds beef stewing cubes

2 tablespoons vegetable oil

1 onion, chopped

2 tart apples (such as Granny Smith), peeled and chopped

1 tablespoon dark brown sugar

1 teaspoon salt

½ teaspoon freshly ground black pepper

2 pounds sandwich steaks (very thinly sliced chuck)

1 tablespoon all-purpose flour

¼ cup apple juice

¾ cup chicken broth

1. Preheat the oven to 350°F. Spray a large skillet with cooking spray and sear the beef cubes over high heat until crusty brown, about 3 to 5 minutes per side. Transfer the cubes to a large plate.

2. Add the oil to the pan. Add the onion, apples, brown sugar, salt, and pepper. Drain any accumulated juices from the beef cubes into the pan, and reserve the cubes to throw into your next stew or soup. Cook over medium heat, stirring frequently and scraping up the browned bits on the bottom of the pan, until the mixture is well browned, about 15 minutes. Turn off the heat. Place

If you can't find sandwich steaks, buy a chuck roast and slice it thinly against the grain. The smallest roasts are usually about 3 pounds, so you can estimate ⅔ or use ½ of a 4-pound roast.

about a tablespoon of the mixture on a strip of steak, about 1 inch from the edge. Roll up the steak strip, starting from the length, and place seam-side down in an 8- or 9-inch square baking dish. Repeat with the remaining steaks. Reserve the leftover filling.

3. Raise the heat to medium-high and sprinkle the remaining filling with the flour. Stir to combine. Whisk in the apple juice and chicken broth and cook until thickened and bubbling. Pour over the stuffed steaks. Cover tightly and bake for 2 hours.

Serves 6 (about 3 stuffed steaks per person)

FOOD FOR THE PRISONERS

· *Roast Beef Sandwiches* · *Ginger Beer* ·

The victors were kind to their prisoners; they locked them up, but they fed them well with "beef and beer" (*Prince Caspian*, chapter 15).

·❧[ROAST BEEF SANDWICHES 🥄🥄🥄]❧·

Of course, everyone knows about the fourth Earl of Sandwich, John Montagu, who was so obsessed with his gambling that he didn't want to leave to have his meals. He took them at the game in the form that became known as a sandwich. This efficient way of carrying food around became so popular that today, whole restaurant chains like Subway devote themselves to selling sandwiches.

2 tablespoons oil
1 onion, sliced
8 thin slices roast beef (you can use
  leftovers from the braised beef; see
  page 91)

8 slices sandwich bread
English mustard
4 large lettuce leaves
8 thin tomato slices

1. Heat the oil in a medium skillet and add the sliced onion. Cook over medium-high heat, stirring often, until the onion is caramelized, about 20 minutes. Set aside to cool.

2. When the onion is cool, prepare the sandwiches. Spread a slice of bread with the English mustard. Lay a lettuce leaf over the mustard and place 2 tomato slices over the lettuce. Place 2 slices of beef over the tomato and spread a quarter of the caramelized onion over the beef. Lay a second slice of bread over the onions and slice the sandwich in half diagonally to form triangles. Repeat to make 4 sandwiches.

Makes 4 sandwiches

⬦❈ Ginger Beer ❈⬦

Serve the sandwiches with ginger beer (see the recipe from the "The Sweets They Had in Those Days" menu on page 41).

DINNER ON THE ISLAND WITHOUT EUSTACE

· Roasted "Goat" (Pan-Seared Strip Steak with Caramelized Onions) ·

Where has Eustace gone? The others have no idea that that spoiled brat is about to have a life-changing experience as they roast and eat some wild goats shot by the archers in their company (*The Voyage of the Dawn Treader*, chapter 6).

ROASTED "GOAT" (PAN-SEARED STRIP STEAK WITH CARAMELIZED ONIONS)

Although many cultures around the world eat goat, it is not commonly found in your local supermarket. In England and the United States, goats are mostly used to produce milk and cheese. This recipe substitutes strip steak.

2 tablespoons vegetable oil

1 onion, sliced

¼ teaspoon salt, plus more for sprinkling

1 pound strip steak

Salt, for sprinkling

Freshly ground black pepper, for sprinkling

½ cup dry red wine

1 cup beef broth

1 garlic clove, minced

2 tablespoons brown sugar

1. Heat the oil in a large skillet. Add the onion and ¼ teaspoon salt. Cook over high heat, stirring, until the onions are well browned, about 10 minutes. Transfer to a large plate.

2. Sprinkle both sides of the steak evenly with salt and pepper and add it to the skillet. Sear over high heat until both sides are crusty brown and the inside registers 140°F, 4 to 5 minutes per side. Transfer to a separate large plate.

3. Add the wine and beef broth to deglaze the pan. Add the garlic and brown

sugar. Cook until the mixture is reduced to about ⅔ cup. Taste and adjust the seasoning.

4. Slice the steak thinly against the grain. Arrange the onions on top and pour the pan sauce over. Serve with rice or wide egg noodles.

Serves 4

DINNER WITH THE DUFFLEPUDS

· *Hearty Mushroom Soup* ·

· *Braised Herb Chicken with Chunky Vegetable Sauce* ·*Hot Boiled Ham* ·

· *Curds and Whey* ·

· *Milk, Cream, Gooseberries, and Red Currants* ·

On Caspian's quest to find the Seven Lost Lords of Narnia, the children and crew find an island full of invisible creatures who they later discover are called Dufflepuds. The Dufflepuds wine and dine them magnificently—although Eustace later regrets having drunk the mead (*The Voyage of the Dawn Treader*, chapter 10).

·❧ HEARTY MUSHROOM SOUP ❧·

The first-century Greek physician Dioscorides believed that mushrooms spontaneously generate, owing to their tendency to spring up suddenly overnight. Witches and fairies are associated with the poisonous toadstool (a red, white-spotted mushroom), which causes hallucinations. But no fear! Mushrooms do not spontaneously generate, and there's no chance that the ones you buy are poisonous.

¼ cup vegetable oil	¼ cup all-purpose flour
1 onion, chopped	6 cups chicken broth
10 ounces mushrooms, sliced	Salt, to taste
2 garlic cloves, minced	Freshly ground black pepper, to taste

1. Heat the oil in a large saucepan and add the onion and mushrooms. Cook over medium-high heat, stirring occasionally, until the water evaporates, 5 to 10 minutes. Continue cooking, stirring frequently, until the mixture browns,

another 5 to 7 minutes. Add the garlic and cook, stirring, just until fragrant, about 30 seconds. Add the flour and stir until combined. Add the chicken broth and stir to combine. Add the salt and pepper.

2. Bring the mixture to a boil, and then reduce to a simmer. Cook, stirring occasionally, about 15 minutes. Remove from the heat. Puree the soup in a blender in batches, or use an immersion blender to puree the soup.

Serves 6

·☙ BRAISED HERB CHICKEN WITH CHUNKY VEGETABLE SAUCE 🍴🥄 ❧·

The Dufflepuds served boiled chicken. The problem with boiling chicken, however, is that the flavor boils out. To preserve flavor, this recipe uses the braising method, in which the chicken slowly cooks in a small amount of liquid, concentrating its flavor rather than diluting it.

4 chicken thighs, patted dry
1 onion, chopped
2 celery ribs, chopped
2 medium carrots, chopped
10 ounces mushrooms, sliced
2 garlic cloves, minced
1 tablespoon all-purpose flour

2 cups chicken broth
Salt, to taste
Freshly ground black pepper, to taste
Dried thyme, for sprinkling over the chicken
Dried rosemary, for sprinkling over the chicken

1. Spray a large, wide pot (such as a Dutch oven) with cooking spray. Sear the chicken thighs, 2 pieces at a time, starting with the skin side, over high heat on both sides until crusty brown, 2 to 3 minutes per side. Remove to a large plate.

2. Pour off all but about 2 tablespoons of the chicken fat. Reduce the heat to medium-high and add the onion, celery, carrots, and mushrooms. Cook, stirring to scrape up the flavorful browned bits on the bottom of the pot. Raise the heat to high and cook, stirring occasionally, until the water cooks out, 5 to 10 minutes. Continue to cook over medium-high heat, stirring frequently, until the vegetable mixture browns, about 10 minutes. Add the garlic and stir until fragrant, a few seconds.

3. Sprinkle the flour over the mixture and stir to combine. Pour in the broth, and stir until smooth. Taste and adjust the seasoning with the salt and pepper (if the broth is salty, you may not need to add salt at all).

4. Lay the chicken over the sauce and pour in any accumulated juices. Sprinkle the tops evenly with the thyme and rosemary. Reduce the heat to a low simmer, cover, and cook until tender, 1½ to 2 hours. Stir occasionally to prevent sticking.

5. Serve the chicken with the chunky sauce poured over it. Pass around more sauce on the side.

Serves 4

·⊰[HOT BOILED HAM]⊱·

Use the recipe from the "On the Run with the Beavers" menu on page 49 for the ham, which was part of the huge meal the Dufflepuds served our heroes.

·⊰[CURDS AND WHEY ⨏⨏⨏]⊱·

Most of us know the nursery rhyme about Little Miss Muffet, who sat on her tuffet, eating her curds and whey. But few of us have ever stopped to consider what a tuffet is (it's an old word for a low stool), or what Miss Muffet was actually eating. Curds and whey, or junket, as it is also called, has an old pedigree. Rennet, the lining of the stomach of certain animals, was added to milk. This makes the milk curdle, thus separating it into curds and whey. The curdled milk was often sweetened and spiced and eaten as dessert. The result, when I tried it, was a watery pudding that looked curdled—because it was—and though the flavor was good, we modern folks accustomed to starch-thickened vanilla pudding will find the texture odd. But I had to try it at least once in my life, if only to know what Miss Muffet was eating and what the Narnia characters enjoyed at the meal the Dufflepuds provided.

2 cups whole milk

¼ cup sugar

1 teaspoon pure vanilla extract

Liquid rennet, as needed (see sidebar)

Ground nutmeg, for dusting

1. Place the milk, sugar, and vanilla in a medium saucepan. Clip a candy thermometer to the side of the pan and cook over medium heat, stirring constantly to dissolve the sugar, until the mixture reaches 98°F. Remove the pan from the heat and stir in the rennet. The mixture will begin to thicken immediately.

2. Pour the curds and whey into a serving dish or into 4 small dessert dishes and leave at room temperature to cool. It will be fully set when it cools to room temperature, about 1 hour. Lightly dust with nutmeg before serving.

You can order liquid rennet in small amounts online. Because rennet comes in different strengths, you will need to experiment to see how much you need. The rennet I used required 2 teaspoons. Interestingly, milk has a saturation point at which more rennet won't make the curds more firm.

Serves 4

·≈[MILK, cream, gooseberries, and red currants]≈·

When you prepare this huge meal, pass around milk to drink and pitchers of cream to pour on everything, because cream improves the flavor of just about everything. Red currants are almost impossible to find in the United States, and gooseberries aren't too easy to find either. Put out bowls of blueberries and cherries or other fresh fruit as an eye-catching and appealing substitute.

LUCY'S LUNCH FROM THE MAGICIAN

· Vegetable–Cheese Omelet ·Cold Lamb ·
· Oniony, Garlicky Pease Porridge ·Strawberry Ice ·
· Lemon Squash · Hot Chocolate ·

For the sake of making the Dufflepuds visible again, Lucy braves the terrifying upstairs—in daylight, of course. She discovers that the evil magician is in fact a kindly old man, and he conjures up a lovely lunch for her (*The Voyage of the Dawn Treader*, chapter 11).

·◦⟧ VEGETABLE-CHEESE OMELET ⟦◦·

Omelets, from the French *omelette*, have been around since at least the Middle Ages; it's a variation on a type of egg dish that originated in Persia. The French, of course, refined it, and the following recipe from a 1653 French cookbook called *Le Patissier françois*, translated by Robert May, is typical even for a modern omelet:

Break six, eight, or ten eggs more or less, beat them together in a dish, and put salt to them; then put some butter a melting in a frying pan, and fry it more or less, according to your discretion, only on one side or bottom.

The one difference is that today, just a couple of eggs are fried at a time, more or less, to make individual portions.

FILLING

3 tablespoons vegetable oil

1 onion, chopped

10 ounces mushrooms, sliced

½ green pepper, chopped

½ *red pepper, chopped*
Salt, to taste
Freshly ground black pepper, to taste

OMELET

4 teaspoons butter, for greasing the
pan
8 large eggs
Salt, to taste

Shredded mild Cheddar cheese, for
filling

Freshly ground black pepper, to taste
1 to 2 tablespoons chopped fresh
chives, for sprinkling

1. To prepare the filling, heat the oil in a skillet and add all the filling ingredients except for the cheese. Cook over medium-high heat, stirring occasionally, until the water cooks out and the vegetables brown, about 20 minutes. Set aside.

2. Heat 1 teaspoon of butter over medium-high heat in a 12-inch skillet. Working with 2 eggs at a time, beat the eggs with salt and pepper and pour into the pan. Swirl the pan to distribute the egg evenly over the surface. Cook until the egg is just set, then slide onto a plate. Place a quarter of the filling on one side, sprinkle some shredded Cheddar cheese over the filling, and fold over. Sprinkle the chopped fresh chives on top. Repeat with the remaining eggs.

Serves 4

··ᴈ[COLD LAMB]ᴈ··

There are two recipes for lamb chops in this book, neither of which I recommend eating cold. Lucy had no choice, but you do! Try the recipes from the "The White Witch's Extravagant Lunch in Our World" menu on page 108 or the "Arguing with Fledge" menu on page 113.

··ᴈ[ONIONY, GARLICKY PEASE PORRIDGE 🥄🥄🥄]ᴈ··

Lucy had green peas for lunch, and pease porridge is an old English way to eat them. Peas were a staple food of the peasant class in medieval

England. Most families had pretty much one cooking utensil, a large cauldron hanging over the fire, into which whatever available food was thrown in. The cauldron could be kept continuously on the fire, with ingredients added as needed, giving new understanding to the nursery rhyme "Pease porridge hot, pease porridge cold, pease porridge in the pot nine days old."

2 tablespoons vegetable oil
1 onion, chopped
2 large or 3 medium garlic cloves,
    minced

1 cup dried split peas, rinsed and
    drained
4 cups chicken broth
Salt, to taste
Freshly ground black pepper, to taste

1. Heat the oil in a medium saucepan and add the onion. Cook over medium-high heat, stirring frequently, until browned. Add the garlic and cook, stirring, until fragrant, about 30 seconds.

2. Add the split peas and chicken broth and bring to a boil. Reduce the heat to low and simmer, covered, for 1½ hours, stirring occasionally to prevent scorching, until very thick. As the porridge thickens, you will need to stir more frequently. Taste and adjust seasoning with salt and pepper.

Serves 4

·≈[STRAWBERRY ICE ♪♪♪]ɔ··

Use the recipe from the "Aravis and Lasaraleen Have a Snack" menu on page 62 as a refreshing complement to the hearty meal the magician prepared for Lucy.

·≈[LEMON SQUASH ♪♪♪]ɔ··

A squash is a type of drink made by mixing a fruit-flavored syrup with water. Although popular in England and other countries, it is not available in the United States. However, it's very simple to make. And I rather suspect that the homemade stuff, made with fresh ingredients and no additives, tastes better anyway.

6 lemons   *½ cup water*
1 cup sugar

1. Peel the zest from 4 of the lemons using a vegetable peeler. Juice all the lemons. Place the zest, lemon juice, and sugar in a small saucepan and bring to a simmer, stirring to dissolve the sugar. Simmer for 30 minutes.
2. Remove from the heat and pour through a sieve into a container. Discard the zest and pulp and stir in the water. Store in the refrigerator until ready to use, up to 4 weeks.
3. Mix ¾ cup of the lemon squash syrup with 3 cups of water to serve.

Makes about 1¼ cups syrup, which makes close to 2 quarts lemon squash

·∙≻[HOT CHOCOLATE]≺∙·

Use the recipe from the "Drink from Trufflehunter the Badger" menu on page 67 for a comforting finish to Lucy's lunch.

Supper for Jill and Eustace at Cair Paravel

· *Hearty Chicken–Rice–Vegetable Soup* ·

· *Pavenders (Grilled Rainbow Smelts)* ·

· *Rack of Venison with Preserved Cherry Port Sauce* · *Peacock* ·

· *Apple Pie* · *Mucky Mouth Pie* · *Fruit Ices* · *Strawberry Jelly* ·

· *Fruit Drinks* · *Ginger Beer, Lemon Squash, and Wines* ·

Jill and Eustace are having a perfectly beastly row when the call to supper interrupts. And what a supper! The two children have never in their lives seen anything like it (*The Silver Chair*, chapter 3).

For the general descriptions of soups, pies, ices, jellies, and drinks, I've selected classic recipes that reflect food that would have been familiar to Jill and Eustace. The exception is peacock. This bird, with its splendid plumage, graced the royal tables at feasts in the past. It was roasted, and cooks would place the bird's feathers back on to make it look impressive (I hope they washed those feathers well first!). However, peacocks disappeared from menus almost as soon as turkeys were introduced to Europe in the sixteenth century. And for good reason: peacocks may look splendid stuffed and roasted and redressed in their feathers, but their meat is tough and stringy.

·⟩∣ Hearty Chicken-Rice-Vegetable Soup ∤ ∤ ∣⟨·

This is one meal in a pot, the way the medieval peasants had it, though they were lucky if they could find a bit of meat to throw into the cauldron. Soup is a descendant of the pottage, the thick stew that made up the peasant's main diet. When all you have is a cauldron to cook with, that's pretty much all you can make. But with different herbs and vegetables, the peasants were able to make endless variations on a grand old theme.

2 chicken breasts, bone-in, skin-on
2 tablespoons vegetable oil, if
necessary
1 onion, chopped
2 medium carrots, chopped
2 celery ribs, chopped

10 ounces mushrooms, sliced
6 cups chicken broth
½ cup long-grain white rice
½ cup chopped fresh parsley
Salt, to taste
Freshly ground black pepper, to taste

1. Sear the chicken over high heat in a Dutch oven or wide pot, skin side first, until both sides are crusty brown, about 3 minutes per side. Transfer to a large plate.

2. If little to no fat has been rendered, add the oil to the pot. Add the onion, carrots, celery, and mushrooms. Cook over medium-high heat, stirring to scrape up the browned bits on the bottom of the pot, until the water is cooked out, about 10 minutes. Continue cooking, stirring frequently, until the mixture is browned, about 10 minutes. Add the broth, rice, parsley, salt, and pepper. Add the chicken breasts, along with any accumulated juices. Bring to a boil, then reduce to a simmer and cook until the chicken is tender, about 30 minutes.

3. Remove the chicken from the pot, discard the skin and bones, and chop into bite-size pieces. Return the chicken to the pot.

Serves 6 to 8

·•⋽[PAVENDERS (GRILLED RAINBOW SMELTS) 🥄🥄🥄]c•··

THANKS TO CHEF CHRIS KOCH FOR THIS RECIPE.

Pavenders are those beautiful rainbow-colored fish found only in Narnia. We ordinary humans will have to make do with rainbow smelt.

2 pounds rainbow smelt, or other
smelt if rainbow is not available
Salt, to taste
Freshly ground black pepper, to taste

¼ cup olive oil

1. Preheat the grill to high if using gas, or fire the charcoal until mostly gray in appearance. Place the smelt on a piece of foil. Season with salt and pepper and drizzle with olive oil.

2. Fold the sides of the foil to the middle and crimp to seal. With a fork, poke a few holes in the top of the foil. Place the foiled smelt on the grill for 5 to 6 minutes. Open the foil, remove the smelt, and serve.

Serves 4

·⊰[Rack of Venison with Preserved Cherry Port Sauce ❘ ❘ ❘]⊱·

THANKS TO CHEF CHRIS KOCH FOR THIS RECIPE.

This recipe calls for a sauce called demi-glace. Demi-glace is made by first cooking a sauce called *espagnole*, which is a basic brown sauce. More stock is added, and the sauce is then reduced to make the demi-glace. To make the espagnole, the classic combination of carrots, celery, and onion known as a *mirepoix* is used.

SAUCE ESPAGNOLE/DEMI-GLACE

1 tablespoon clarified butter (see sidebar)

1 tablespoon minced carrots

1 tablespoon minced celery

2 tablespoons minced onion

1½ tablespoons all-purpose flour

1½ cup brown stock or beef stock, divided

1 teaspoon tomato paste

⅛ bunch fresh flat-leaf parsley

1 bay leaf

1. Heat the clarified butter in a small saucepan over medium-high heat and add the carrots, celery, and onion. Brown the mirepoix in the butter, about 10 minutes, stirring constantly to prevent scorching. Stir in the flour and cook to a deep brown, about another 10 minutes, stirring constantly to prevent scorching.

2. Reduce the heat to medium, whisk in ¾ cup brown stock, and stir over medium heat until smooth. Add the tomato paste, parsley, and bay leaf and simmer over the lowest possible heat, covered, for 10 minutes. Strain into a bowl, wipe the

pan clean, and return the sauce to the pan. Add the remaining ½ cup brown stock and simmer to reduce to ¼ cup of demi-glace. Set aside.

RACK OF VENISON

1 cup breadcrumbs

1 clove garlic, minced

2 tablespoons minced fresh thyme

2 juniper berries, crushed (see sidebar)

2 tablespoons extra-virgin olive oil

1 (8-bone) rack of red deer (if using fallow deer, use 2 racks, 1 rack for every two portions)

1 cup port

¼ cup demi-glace

1 cup preserved cherries (see sidebar)

1. Preheat the oven to 375°F. In a mixing bowl, combine the breadcrumbs, garlic, thyme, juniper berries, and oil and mix well. Coat the racks with the breadcrumb mixture and place on a rack in a roasting pan. Roast for 45 minutes, or until the internal temperature registers 140°F for medium rare. Remove and tent with foil to keep warm.

2. Pour out the fat from the roasting pan and add the port. Place the roasting pan over a burner and bring to a simmer over medium-high heat, scraping up the browned bits from the bottom with a wooden spoon. Add the demi-glace and preserved cherries and heat through. Carve the rack and serve two chops each, with sauce drizzled over the meat.

You can replace the clarified butter with an equal amount of vegetable oil, but not with whole butter. Otherwise, to make clarified butter, place at least 4 ounces of butter in a double boiler or heatproof bowl over boiling water. The butter will melt into three layers: scum (whey), fat, and milk. Skim off the scum (white foam) and refrigerate the remaining layers. The milk will sink to the bottom. When the mixture is solid, remove the layer of clarified fat from the top. This yellow layer of fat is the clarified butter that you will use. The remaining milk can be used in other recipes as buttermilk, or it can be discarded. Clarified butter is useful for cooking as it doesn't burn as easily as butter. But if you're not going to be using it in other recipes, replace it with the suggested alternative.

Juniper berries can be found in the spice aisle or at specialty food stores. They can also be ordered online.

Preserved cherries can sometimes be found in the gourmet section of the supermarket. Otherwise, you can substitute cherry preserves, which can be found near the jams and jellies.

Serves 4

·⊰[PEACOCK]⊱·

Use the classic roast turkey recipe from the "Dinner from the Giants" menu on page 163 for this dish.

·⊰[APPLE PIE 🍴🍴🍴]⊱·

Check out this recipe for apple pie from around 1390, created by King Richard II's cooks and collected in a book called the *Forme of Cury*:

For to make tarts in apples. Take good apples and good spices and figs and raisins and pears, and when they are well brayed [pounded], colored with saffron well, and do it in a coffin [pie crust] and do it forth to bake well. [Spelling and punctuation have been changed to make the text easier to read.]

Hey, they forgot the sugar! But besides that, this is recognizable more than six hundred years later as an apple pie.

PIE DOUGH
2½ cups all-purpose flour
3 tablespoons sugar
½ teaspoon salt

16 tablespoons (1 cup) butter, chilled
   and cut into chunks
½ to ¾ cup ice water, as needed

APPLE FILLING
2 pounds apples (about 8),
   combination of sweet and tart,
   such as Braeburn and Granny
   Smith, peeled, cored, and sliced
¾ cup light brown sugar
1 teaspoon ground cinnamon
⅛ teaspoon ground nutmeg
Grated zest and juice of 1 lemon

1 egg, beaten with 1 tablespoon
   water, for brushing over the pie
2 tablespoons turbinado sugar,
   granulated sugar, or cinnamon
   sugar for sprinkling over the pie

1. To make the pie dough, place the flour, sugar, and salt in a food processor and pulse a few seconds until combined. Scatter the butter pieces over the flour and pulse until the mixture resembles a coarse yellow meal, about 15 pulses. Turn out into a large mixing bowl, sprinkle ½ cup water on top, and fold with a rubber spatula until the dough adheres together. If the dough is dry, add water 1 tablespoon at a time (better too wet than too dry). Divide the dough in half, shape into 2 disks, wrap in plastic wrap, and chill at least 2 hours or up to 3 days.

    > You can use frozen prerolled dough to save time.

2. While the dough is chilling, place the apples, brown sugar, cinnamon, nutmeg, and lemon zest and juice in a large pot. Cook, stirring occasionally, until the juices are released. Drain the apples and spread on a baking sheet to cool quickly.

3. When you are ready to assemble the pie, adjust the oven rack to the lowest position, place a heavy baking sheet on the rack, and preheat the oven to 350°F. On a floured work surface, roll out 1 disk of dough to ⅛-inch thick (if the dough is too hard to roll out, leave it out to soften for 15 minutes or so). Fold the dough in quarters, brushing off the excess flour after each fold, and unfold into a 9-inch pie pan. Pour the apple filling into the shell.

4. Roll out the second disk ⅛-inch thick. Fold in quarters, brushing off the excess flour after each fold, and unfold over the filling. Trim the overhang to 1 inch all around and tuck under. Crimp the edges with your fingers or use a fork to seal. If desired, cut out shapes such as leaves from the scraps of dough, and stick to the pie with a bit of water to decorate the pie.

5. Brush the beaten egg over the pie and sprinkle with the desired type of sugar. Cut slits for vents. Place the pie on the baking sheet in the oven and bake for about 1½ hours, until the crust is golden and juices are bubbling. Cool to room temperature before serving, or serve warm with custard. (Use the Warm Custard Sauce recipe from the Jam Roly Poly with Custard in the "High Tea after Battle" menu on page 57.)

Serves 8

❧ MUCKY MOUTH PIE ✦✦✦ ❧

I came across this pie while researching traditional pies that would have been familiar to Jill and Eustace, and I fell in love with its quaint name. The pie is supposed to be made with bilberries, a close relative of blueberries that stains the teeth and mouth, hence the name "mucky mouth." Because bilberries aren't available in the United States, this pie uses blueberries instead. This is an iced pie, a strange but interesting British tradition where the pie is slathered with royal icing shortly before it finishes baking and is then returned to the oven to harden.

PIE DOUGH

2 cups all-purpose flour

2 tablespoons sugar

½ teaspoon salt

12 tablespoons (¾ cup) butter or

margarine, chilled and cut into chunks

½ cup ice water, plus more as needed

FILLING

2 tart apples, such as Granny Smith, peeled, cored, and sliced

½ cup loosely packed fresh mint leaves

1½ pounds (about 5 cups) blueberries

Juice of 1 lemon

1 cup sugar

¼ cup cornstarch

ROYAL ICING

2 large egg whites, at room temperature

2 cups confectioners' sugar

> If you want to skip the icing, then before baking, brush the top of the pie with 1 egg beaten with 1 tablespoon water. Sprinkle with turbinado sugar or granulated sugar and bake as directed.

1. To make the dough, process the flour, sugar, and salt for a few seconds in the food processor until just combined. Scatter the chunks of butter or margarine over the flour mixture and pulse just until the mixture resembles a coarse yellow meal, with larger bits of fat remaining, about 15 pulses. Turn the mixture out into a large mixing bowl, drizzle the water over, and toss with a rubber spatula until the dough begins to clump together. Add

more water 1 tablespoon at a time if the dough is too dry (better too wet than too dry). Divide the dough in half, form into disks, wrap in plastic wrap, and chill in the refrigerator at least 2 hours or up to 3 days.

2. To make the filling, process the apples and mint leaves in a food processor until smooth. Scrape into a large saucepan and add the blueberries, lemon juice, sugar, and cornstarch. Toss to combine. Cook over medium-high heat, stirring frequently, until thickened and bubbling, about 10 minutes. Remove from the heat and cool to room temperature.

3. Adjust the oven rack to the lowest position and place a heavy baking sheet on the rack. Preheat the oven to 350°F. To assemble the pie, roll out 1 disk of dough (if one is slightly larger, use that one) on a floured work surface to form a 12-inch circle. Fold the dough in quarters, brushing off the excess flour with a pastry brush after each fold. Unfold the dough into a 9-inch pie pan. Place the filling into the shell. Roll out the second disk of dough to form an 11-inch circle. Fold the dough into quarters, brushing off the excess flour with a pastry brush after each fold. Then place over the filling. Trim the overhang to about ½ inch over the rim of the pie dish. Fold the edges under and crimp with a fork or flute with your fingers to seal. Cut slits for vents. Carefully place the pie on the baking sheet and bake for 1½ hours, until golden brown. Remove the pie from the oven and cool slightly while preparing the royal icing. Leave the oven on.

4. To make the royal icing, beat the egg whites until soft mounds form. Add the confectioners' sugar slowly, scraping down the sides often, and beat until thick enough to spread. Use about ⅔ of the icing to cover the pie just up to the crimped or fluted border. You will not need all the icing, but it's hard to make a smaller amount. Place the pie in the oven and bake another 10 minutes, until the icing hardens. Cool completely before slicing the pie, or else the filling will ooze. The royal icing will shatter when you slice the pie.

Serves 8

·∙]̊ꞮꞲuꞮꞇ Ɪꞓes ♪♪♪]̊∙·

Icing fruit juices and wines goes back thousands of years, when people brought snow down from the mountaintops for this purpose. The Romans (not the common citizens, of course, but rather the upper classes) enjoyed snow mixed with honey and dried fruit. The Arabs in the Middle East are credited with inventing sherbet, which comes from the Arab word *sharbât* (the root of the word *sorbet*, as well). You will need an ice cream maker for this recipe and the one that follows.

BLUEBERRY SORBET

2 pounds (about 7 cups) blueberries,
  fresh or frozen, thawed if frozen
1½ cups sugar

Juice of 1 lemon
1 cup water

1. Place the blueberries, sugar, lemon juice, and water in the bowl of a food processor. Process until smooth, 1 or 2 minutes.

2. Push the mixture through a sieve with a rubber spatula, stirring and pressing to extract as much juice as possible. Discard the pulp. Chill until cold.

3. Freeze in an ice cream maker according to the manufacturer's instructions. Transfer to an airtight container and freeze until firm.

4. Soften at room temperature for 15 minutes before serving.

Makes about 5 cups

PEACH SORBET

Using frozen peaches rather than fresh saves you the bother of having to peel the peaches and— worst of all—trying to detach them from the stones if they are the clingstone rather than the freestone variety. Unfortunately, you can't tell which kind you're buying at your typical grocery store.

2 (16-ounce) bags frozen sliced peaches, thawed
1½ cups sugar
Juice of 2 lemons
1½ cups water

1. Place all the ingredients in a food processor or blender and process until smooth. Pour through a sieve, pushing and scraping with a rubber spatula until every last bit of juice

possible is extracted. Discard the pulp and transfer the puree to a container. Chill until very cold, about 5 hours.

2. Freeze in an ice cream maker according to the manufacturer's instructions.

Makes about 6 cups

·❧ STRAWBERRY JELLY 🥄🥄🥄 ❧·

Jellies in Victorian times were made from calf's foot gelatin or isinglass from the bladders of sturgeon (try not to think too much about that). They were poured into fancy molds, as they often are today, as well. Some food artists of the time made elaborate creations that were truly works of art, creating scenes made out of food inside a globe of jelly.

4 teaspoons (about 1½ packets)
   powdered gelatin
½ cup water

1 pound strawberries
½ cup sugar
Juice of 1 lemon

1. Sprinkle the gelatin over the water in a bowl and leave to soften. Process the strawberries with the sugar and lemon juice in a blender or food processor until smooth. Push through a sieve using a rubber spatula. Discard the seeds and pulp.

2. Cook the strawberry mixture in a medium saucepan over medium-high heat, stirring occasionally, until hot and bubbling. Whisk in the gelatin mixture. Continue whisking several minutes, until completely dissolved. Pour into a bowl, cool to room temperature, and chill until set, 5 to 6 hours or overnight.

Serves 6

·❧ FRUIT DRINKS ❧·

FRUIT PUNCH 🥄🥄🥄

2 cups apple juice
1 cup pineapple juice
1 cup white grape juice

1 teaspoon orange extract
Red food coloring, optional

1. Mix all the ingredients together, including the red food coloring, if desired.
2. Chill until cold.

Makes 1 quart

STRAWBERRY-BANANA-ORANGE DRINK 🥄🥄🥄

*1 pound strawberries, washed, leafy
  crowns removed*
*1 medium ripe banana, cut into
  chunks*
2 cups orange juice

1 cup white grape juice
¾ cup sugar
*2 teaspoons strawberry flavor,
  optional*

1. Process all the ingredients in a blender or food processor until smooth.
2. Pour through a sieve, scraping with a rubber spatula if necessary.
3. Chill until cold and mix well before serving.

Makes about 5 cups

⊶⊱ GINGER BEER, LEMON SQUASH, AND WINES ⊰⊷

Serve this dinner with ginger beer and lemon squash (recipes on pages 41 and 148) and a couple of nice wines for the adults.

DINNER WITH PUDDLEGLUM

· Eel Stew ·

I just love Puddleglum! He is so delightfully gloomy. He's sure the children won't like the eel stew, and when they ask for second helpings, he's sure that if they really do like it, then it will make them sick. Surely something is bound to go wrong (*The Silver Chair*, chapter 5)! Use the eel stew recipe from "Packing for the Road with Puddleglum" on page 74.

DINNER FROM THE GIANTS

· Cock-a-Leekie Soup ·Roasted Herbed Turkey Breast ·
· Steamed Bread and Butter Pudding · Roast Chestnuts ·

What a relief! Jill is tired and footsore, and a giant bath is just the thing she needs—followed by a delicious hot supper provided by a slightly irritating giantess nurse who keeps calling her "poppet" and who kisses her as she tucks her into bed. C. S. Lewis acknowledges that being kissed by a giantess is not pleasant, but Jill is so tired and so contented after her hot supper, followed by "as much fruit as you could eat," that she falls asleep almost immediately (*The Silver Chair*, chapter 8).

·◄[COCK-A-LEEKIE SOUP]►·

This Scottish specialty dates back to a time when a sport called cockfighting was popular. The losing cock—which was dead, of course—was cooked into a soup with leeks, which the sports lovers enjoyed. A major debate erupted over whether to include prunes or not. The early nineteenth-century French diplomat Talleyrand settled the matter by suggesting that the prunes be cooked with the soup and removed before serving. Prunes are included in this version; they give the soup a lovely color, and you'd never guess you're eating prunes (just don't tell anyone they're in there).

4 chicken thighs, about 2½ pounds
1 onion, chopped
2 quarts chicken broth
1 bunch leeks, chopped
½ cup chopped prunes

2 cloves garlic, minced
½ cup pearled barley
½ teaspoon freshly ground black
* pepper*
Salt, to taste

1. Spray a Dutch oven or wide pot with cooking spray and sear the chicken thighs over high heat on both sides, skin side first, until golden and the fat is rendered, 3 to 5 minutes per side. Work in batches if needed. Transfer the chicken to a large plate and pour off most of the chicken fat from the pot.

2. Add the onion and cook over medium heat, scraping up the browned bits, until the onion is browned. Add the broth and the remaining ingredients, except for the salt. Add the chicken to the pot, along with any accumulated juices. Bring to a simmer and cook for 1½ hours, until the chicken and barley are tender. Skim off the fat every so often as the soup cooks.

3. Remove the chicken from the pot. Remove the skin and bones and cut the chicken into bite-size pieces. Return the chicken to the pot. Taste and adjust seasoning with salt.

Serves 6 to 8

ROASTED HERBED TURKEY BREAST

My favorite turkey legend is the way turkeys were transported from Norfolk and Suffolk to London. It was a long walk, so to prevent their feet from getting sore, they were outfitted with little booties. Imagine huge flocks of turkeys trotting along wearing little shoes on their feet. Life was made easier—and shorter—for the poor birds when advances in shipping were made.

1 cup water
¼ cup olive oil
1 teaspoon salt
½ teaspoon freshly ground black pepper

½ teaspoon dried sage
½ teaspoon dried rosemary
1 (6- to 7-pound) turkey breast

1. Preheat the oven to 425°F. Fill a large roasting pan set with a V-rack with the water.

2. In a small mixing bowl, combine the oil, salt, pepper, sage, and rosemary and mix well. Carefully slide your fingers under the turkey's skin and separate it from the breast, taking care not to tear it. Rub the outside of the skin and underneath with the oil-herb mixture.

3. Place the turkey breast on the V-rack and roast for 30 minutes. Reduce the heat to 325°F and continue cooking until the meat registers 160°F, about 1 hour longer. Remove the turkey from the oven and allow it to rest for 20 minutes to allow the juices to redistribute before carving it. (The temperature will rise a few degrees due to residual heat.)

Serves 8

⚜ STEAMED BREAD AND BUTTER PUDDING 🥄🥄🥄 ⚜

Steamed puddings have an ancient history, going back to medieval times and beyond when the stomach lining of an animal would be filled with cereal and other ingredients and steamed in a cauldron with the rest of the pottage. Gradually, sweet ingredients were added to the pudding, and in the 1600s, the pudding cloth replaced the animal bladder. Today, pudding molds replace the pudding cloth, making them even easier to make.

Puddings make fans wax poetic, such as Dr. Samuel Johnson, who sang praises to the grain that provided the wheat, the dairy maid who milked the cow, the egg—and even the salt. A French expatriate to England (Francis Maximilian Misson) was just as enthusiastic, calling pudding manna that is better than the biblical stuff, and describing the many and various ways the British prepare the dish (baked, boiled, or with meat).

Thrifty cooks looking to reuse stale bread in a way that would be appealing invented bread pudding, and its popularity is attested to by the seven recipes for bread pudding included in one Victorian cookbook. For this classic recipe, use a rich bread like challah or brioche.

8 to 12 slices of bread, to make enough layers to come within 2 inches of the rim of a 2-quart pudding bowl (see sidebar); no need to remove the crusts unless they are very tough
2 tablespoons butter for spreading on the bread

2½ cups milk
1½ cups heavy cream
2 large eggs
6 large egg yolks
¾ cup sugar
1 tablespoon pure vanilla extract

1. Grease a 2-quart pudding bowl. Spread each slice of bread with butter on one side, neither thickly nor thinly, and layer the slices of bread and butter to come within 2 inches of the rim.

2. Whisk the milk, heavy cream, eggs, egg yolks, sugar, and vanilla in a large mixing bowl until smooth. Pour over the bread and butter. Push the bread down with

a fork to submerge. Let the pudding sit for 2 hours, pushing the bread down with a fork to submerge it from time to time. Fill a large pot with water and place an upside-down saucer or steamer in the pot. Bring to a boil.

3. Cover the bowl with a tight-fitting lid and place it in the pot, making sure the water comes about halfway up the sides. Simmer for 2 hours, taking care not to let the pot boil dry. Remove the pudding bowl from the pot and cool completely before unmolding. To unmold, shake the pudding back and forth to loosen it, then invert it onto a plate.

Serves 8

> Instead of a pudding bowl, you can use a 2-quart glass or stainless steel bowl. Place the covered bowl in a roasting pan and fill the pan with hot water. Cover the whole pan with aluminum foil and place in a 350°F preheated oven. Steam for 2 hours. Remove from the pot and cool completely before unmolding.

·⊰] ROAST CHESTNUTS ⎰⎰⎰ [⊱·

The Greeks brought chestnuts from Asia Minor, but the Romans gave us the recipes. The Romans ground chestnuts into flour and used it as a filler for wheat flour, and the ancient Roman cookbook, *Apicius*, has a recipe for cooking it with lentils. Few things suggest a cozy winter scene, though, more than simple fresh-roasted chestnuts, a fire in the hearth, and friends at the table.

2 pounds chestnuts

1. Preheat the oven to 350°F.
2. Wash the chestnuts well and line them up on a baking sheet. Score an X on each nut with a sharp knife.
3. Roast for 45 to 50 minutes, until the shells peel away and the nuts feel soft when pressed.

Serves 6

LUNCH FROM THE GIANTS

· Cold Venison ·

Oh, horror! Jill is enjoying the nice, tender venison the giants have provided for lunch when Puddleglum stops her cold. He's just discovered that a talking stag was murdered to provide that day's venison. Jill doesn't understand what the fuss is all about, being new to Narnia, but Puddleglum and Eustace feel like cannibals (*The Silver Chair*, chapter 9).

Use the cold roast venison recipe from the "Food for Flight with Prince Caspian" menu on page 64.

PRINCE RILIAN ORDERS FOOD FOR THE UPDWELLERS

· Pigeon and Morel Pie · Cold Ham ·
· Green Salad with Apples and Raisins ·Heavenly Honey Cake ·
· Triple Almond Cake with Raspberry Filling ·

The knight is very strange, but he doesn't forget to order food for his visitors. Before facing the difficult decision of whether to free him or not, our faithful trio enjoy some good food (*The Silver Chair*, chapter 11).

⊷] PIGEON AND MOREL PIE 🥄🥄🥄 [⊶

THANKS TO CHEF CHRIS KOCH FOR THIS RECIPE.

The ingredients for this pie filling are bound up with a velouté, which is a sauce made by thickening stock with a roux. A roux is a paste made with equal parts fat and flour. There are three types: white, blond, and brown. The color depends on how long you cook the roux. The longer you cook it, the deeper the color; and the deeper the color, the deeper the flavor. A brown roux also imparts a slightly nutty flavor to the finished sauce. This recipe calls for a brown roux.

CRUST

3 cups all-purpose flour
½ teaspoon salt
16 tablespoons (1 cup) butter, chilled and cubed

5 tablespoons shortening, chilled and cut into pieces
About 1 cup ice water, more or less as needed

FILLING

5 cups chicken stock

1 ounce dried morel mushrooms

3 pounds pigeon, cut into pieces	3 tablespoons all-purpose flour
2 bay leaves	Salt, to taste
2 russet potatoes, peeled and diced	Freshly ground black pepper, to taste
1 cup pearl onions	1 cup baby peas
3 tablespoons butter	1 egg, lightly beaten

1. To make the crust, sift together the flour and salt. Place the mixture in a bowl and cut in the butter and shortening, or place in the bowl of a food processor and pulse to cut the butter and shortening into the flour. Add enough water to form a dough, wrap in plastic wrap, and refrigerate for 30 minutes.

2. To make the filling, bring the stock to a boil in a large pot. Add the dried mushrooms, stir, and remove from the heat. Let the mushrooms steep for 30 minutes. Remove the mushrooms with a slotted spoon, strain the liquid, and reserve the broth.

3. Place the pigeon, mushroom soaking liquid, and bay leaves into the pot. Bring to a boil. Reduce to a simmer, cover, and simmer for 20 minutes. Remove the pigeon and set aside to cool. Keep the cooking liquid in the pot at a simmer. Remove the bones from the pigeon, shred the meat, and set aside. Add the potatoes to the stock and cook until tender, about 10 minutes. Remove the potatoes with a slotted spoon and set aside.

4. While the potatoes cook, trim the ends of the pearl onions, and cut a shallow X into the root ends. Place in the potato cooking water for 30 seconds and transfer to an ice bath. Gently squeeze the stem end, and the onion should pop out of the bottom.

5. Increase the temperature to high under the stock and boil to reduce to about 2 cups, about 10 minutes; then remove the bay leaf. While the stock reduces, melt the butter in a medium saucepan. Add the flour and cook, stirring, until the roux (the butter-flour mixture) turns brown, about 10 minutes. Add the 2 cups of stock and whisk to create a thick, smooth sauce. Simmer for 10 minutes; then adjust the seasonings with salt and pepper.

6. Preheat the oven to 375°F. Roll out the dough on a floured work surface. Place a layer of dough into a 10-inch deep-dish pie pan and add the pigeon meat, soaked mushrooms, cooked potatoes, onions, and peas. Add the sauce and top with the remaining pastry. Crimp the edges and cut steam holes. Brush the top with a beaten egg and bake at 350°F for one hour. Remove from the oven and let rest for 15 minutes before serving.

Serves 6

·≈] COLD HAM [≈·

Use the recipe from the "On the Run with the Beavers" menu on page 49. Cool the ham before serving.

·≈] GREEN SALAD WITH APPLES AND RAISINS ♂♂♂ [≈·

A seventeenth-century salad recipe calls for arranging sliced capon, olives, samphires (a type of edible coastal-growing plant), broom buds (a type of edible flower), pickled mushrooms, pickled oysters, lemon, orange, raisins, almonds, blue figs, Virginia Potato, caperon (whatever that is), and crucifix pease (peas), and pouring a simple vinaigrette over the whole dish. Call this recipe a super simplified version of the above. Even people who don't like to eat their vegetables enjoy the following recipe—maybe because there's only one vegetable in it.

1 head romaine lettuce (or your
   favorite green leafy vegetable),
   washed and chopped
1 tart apple (such as Granny Smith),
   peeled, cored, and chopped
Juice of 1 lemon
¼ cup pine nuts

¼ cup raisins
2 tablespoons olive oil
1 tablespoon balsamic vinegar
½ teaspoon salt
¼ teaspoon freshly ground black
   pepper

1. Place the lettuce in a large bowl. Toss the apple with the lemon juice and add to the lettuce along with the pine nuts and raisins.

2. Place the olive oil, balsamic vinegar, salt, and pepper in a small jar. Seal and shake vigorously until an emulsion forms, a few seconds. Pour the dressing over the salad, toss, and serve.

Serves 6

·◦⁊ heavenly honey cake 🥄🥄🥄 ⁊◦·

Did you know that archaeologists have discovered honey cake molds at sites in Egypt, Greece, and Rome? So honey cake has a respectably long history. But the gross factor? Honey was used in ancient civilizations like Egypt for embalming dead people. And no wonder: honey, properly sealed, can last several hundred *years*.

2 cups all-purpose flour
1 teaspoon baking powder
½ teaspoon baking soda
¼ teaspoon salt
1 teaspoon ground cinnamon
⅔ cup oil
¾ cup honey
½ cup granulated sugar

¼ cup dark brown sugar
Grated zest and juice of 1 orange
2 large eggs, at room temperature
⅔ cup coffee made with 1 teaspoon
*   instant coffee, cooled to room*
*   temperature*
Confectioners' sugar for dusting,
*   optional*

1. Adjust the oven rack to the middle position and preheat the oven to 325°F. Spray a 9-inch square baking pan with baking spray with flour.

2. In a large mixing bowl, whisk together the flour, baking powder, baking soda, salt, and cinnamon. In a separate bowl, using an electric mixer, beat the oil, honey, granulated sugar, brown sugar, orange zest, and eggs until smooth and fluffy, about 5 minutes, scraping down the sides as necessary. Add the orange juice and mix to combine. Add half the flour mixture and mix on the slowest speed to combine. Add the coffee and stir to combine. Add the remaining flour mixture and stir to combine.

3. Give the batter a final stir with a rubber spatula and scrape it into the prepared pan. Bake for 40 to 45 minutes, rotating the pan halfway through baking, until the cake feels set when touched lightly in the center. You can cool the cake in the pan and serve it right out of the pan. Dust it with confectioners' sugar for a more festive look, if desired.

Makes 1 9-inch square cake

TRIPLE ALMOND CAKE WITH RASPBERRY FILLING ♪ ♪ ♪

Almonds are mentioned in the Bible (Aaron's staff was made of the wood of an almond tree), and these nuts have an enormous number of uses. Besides being a great snack raw or roasted, they're the basis of marzipan and macaroons, they're used in nougat, and almond butter is a good alternative to peanut butter. This cake uses almonds in three different ways to get the most out of the almond flavor.

1½ cups cake flour, sifted
1 cup finely ground almonds
1½ teaspoons baking powder
½ teaspoon baking soda
¼ teaspoon salt
4 eggs, at room temperature
1½ cups granulated sugar
1 teaspoon almond extract

12 tablespoons (¾ cup) butter,
*   melted and cooled slightly*
½ cup whole milk, at room
*   temperature or slightly warmed*
½ cup chopped almonds
1 cup raspberry jam
Confectioners' sugar, for dusting

1. Set the oven rack to the middle position and preheat the oven to 350°F. Grease 2 9-inch round cake pans and line the bottoms with parchment paper.

2. Whisk together the flour, ground almonds, baking powder, baking soda, and salt. In a separate bowl, using an electric mixer fitted with the whisk attachment, whip the eggs, granulated sugar, and almond extract until the volume is tripled and the mixture is very pale, almost white. Slowly drizzle in the melted butter, whipping after each addition until fully incorporated and scraping down the sides as needed. The entire addition of the butter will take several minutes.

3. Add half the flour mixture, mixing on the slowest speed until incorporated. Add the milk, stirring until incorporated. Repeat with the remaining flour. Fold in the chopped almonds by hand with a rubber spatula.

4. Divide the batter between the 2 pans and bake for 30 minutes, until golden. Cool in the pans, then invert the cakes and peel off the parchment paper. Lay one cake, top side down, on a plate or cake platter. Spread the raspberry jam evenly over the cake to within ½ inch of the border. Lay the second cake, top side up, over the filling. Dust with confectioners' sugar.

Serves 16 dieters (who are cheating but trying not to cheat too badly) or 8 hearty eaters

First Meal Back in the Overworld

· Spicy Sausage Patties · Frothy Hot Chocolate ·

· Garlic and Rosemary Roast Potatoes · Roast Chestnuts ·

· Raisin–Stuffed Baked Apples · Strawberry Sorbet · Lemon Ices ·

It is wonderful to be back. Jill wakes up, and after remembering with relief that she's no longer in the gloomy and depressing Underworld, she sleepily recalls the delicious dinner the dwarves provided the previous night (*The Silver Chair*, chapter 16).

·◦⟦ SPICY SAUSAGE PATTIES ⫯⫯⫯ ⟧◦·

We know from the cookbook author Apicius and other sources that as far back as Roman times, people were making sausages. Making your own real sausages is a hassle, what with obtaining casings, stuffing them, and boiling them. So here's a delicious but simple alternative.

2 tablespoons vegetable oil

1 onion, chopped

1½ pounds ground beef

2 large eggs

½ cup seasoned breadcrumbs, or
    breadcrumbs seasoned with salt,
    pepper, and dried parsley, plus
    about 1 cup for coating

1 tablespoon tomato paste

½ teaspoon salt

¼ teaspoon ground cayenne pepper

2 garlic cloves, minced

3 large eggs, beaten, for coating

Vegetable oil for frying

1. Heat the oil in a skillet. Add the onion and cook over medium-high heat, stirring frequently, until browned. Transfer to a large mixing bowl and cool slightly.

2. Add the beef, eggs, ½ cup breadcrumbs, tomato paste, salt, cayenne pepper, and garlic to the mixing bowl. Mix well.

3.   Place the eggs in one bowl and the remaining breadcrumbs in another. Fill a skillet with oil to come a half inch up the sides, and heat. Form the beef mixture into patties. Dip each patty into the eggs and then coat with the breadcrumbs. Fry until golden brown, about 4 minutes per side. Transfer to a paper towel–lined plate to drain.

Makes about 1½ dozen sausage patties

·⊰[Frothy Hot Chocolate]⊱·

Use the hot chocolate recipe from the "Drink from Trufflehunter the Badger" menu on page 67.

·⊰[Garlic and Rosemary Roast Potatoes 🥄🥄🥄]⊱·

In France, dishes that have *parmentier* in the name contain potatoes, in tribute to Antoine-Augustin Parmentier, the French agronomist who persuaded the French to cultivate and eat the potato. He is famous for getting the queen, Marie Antoinette of let-them-eat-cake fame, to wear potato blossoms, and for hiring an armed patrol to guard his potato field, with instructions to allow the curious peasants to sneak in at night to take potatoes to plant in their own gardens. Thus, he was able to prove that potatoes are not poisonous. Indeed, potatoes helped to reduce famine in France toward the end of the eighteenth century.

¼ cup olive oil
3 cloves garlic, minced
1 teaspoon salt
¼ teaspoon freshly ground black pepper

1 teaspoon dried rosemary
3 pounds (about 6 large) red bliss potatoes, unpeeled, scrubbed, and cut into 1-inch cubes

1.   Preheat the oven to 350°F. Combine the olive oil with the garlic, salt, pepper, and rosemary. Toss the potatoes with the oil mixture and turn into a 9-inch-by-13-inch pan. Cover and bake for 1 hour, until the potatoes are soft

and easily pierced with a fork. Uncover and bake another 10 minutes to crisp the potatoes.

Serves 6

·∙⊰[ROAST CHESTNUTS]⊱∙·

Use the Roast Chestnuts recipe on page 165.

·∙⊰[RAISIN-STUFFED BAKED APPLES 🥄🥄🥄]⊱∙·

References to apples in ancient literature, such as King Solomon's *Song of Songs,* may have actually been describing quince. Ancient apples were small, consisted mostly of the core, and were not very good to eat. The Romans discovered how to cultivate apples to produce ones they liked; they learned to graft a branch of the desired apple tree because the seeds themselves often produced very different apples than the parent tree. In the medieval period in England, apples were bred to be larger and were much used in cookery, as they are now.

*4 Golden Delicious apples, cored
   (leave the blossom ends intact; see
   sidebar)*
¼ cup dark brown sugar

¼ cup golden raisins
¼ teaspoon ground cinnamon
⅓ cup water

1. Preheat the oven to 350°F and place the apples in an 8-inch baking dish. Mix the brown sugar, raisins, and cinnamon together and stuff into the cored apples, packing the mixture down to fit in as much filling as possible.

> Use a melon baller to core the apples, beginning at the stem end but leaving the blossom end intact.

2. Pour a little of the water over each apple, just enough to moisten the filling. Pour the rest of the water into the bottom of the pan. Bake for 50 minutes, until the apples are soft to the touch but not bursting open.

Makes 4 baked apples

·⌍[STRAWBERRY SORBET ♪♪♪]⌌·

The Victorians liked to serve ices like sorbet in the middle of an elaborate meal. Guests might have two or three sumptuous courses, a pause
for the ices, and a resumption of the meal. Even today, at some extravagant, upscale dinners, ices may be served in the middle of the meal to
refresh the guests before continuing with the menu. Mostly, however,
sorbet today makes a light, refreshing dessert. You will need an ice
cream maker for this recipe.

2 pounds strawberries, fresh or
*   frozen, thawed if frozen*
1¼ cups sugar

Juice of 2 lemons
1 cup water

1. Place the strawberries, sugar, lemon juice, and water in the bowl of a food processor. Process until smooth, 1 or 2 minutes.
2. Push the mixture through a sieve with a rubber spatula, stirring and pressing to
   extract as much juice as possible. Discard the pulp. Chill until cold.
3. Freeze in an ice cream maker according to the manufacturer's instructions.
   Transfer to an airtight container and freeze until firm.
4. Allow the sorbet to soften at room temperature for 15 minutes before serving.

Makes about 5 cups

·⌍[LEMON ICES ♪♪♪]⌌·

Arabs are credited with discovering lemons and cultivating them for
the first time. Though they were rare and expensive in the Middle Ages
in Europe, in later centuries, they were more easily obtainable and
were used a lot in cooking. And, of course, they were famously given to
British sailors as protection against scurvy.

¼ cup freshly squeezed lemon juice
*   (from about 2 lemons)*
⅓ cup sugar

1 teaspoon lemon extract, optional
Water, as needed

1. Combine the lemon juice, sugar, and lemon extract, if using, in a 2-cup measuring cup. Fill the rest of the way to the 2-cup line with water and mix well.
2. Fill an ice cube tray with the lemon mixture and freeze until firm. Crush 3 to 4 ice cubes at a time in a blender per serving. Scrape into bowls and serve at once.

Makes about 4 servings

THE TALKING BEASTS FEED KING TIRIAN

· Hot Chocolate, Wine, and Cheese · Oatcakes with Fresh Butter ·

King Tirian may have been tied to a tree and left to suffer on "Aslan's" orders, but he is not alone. The Talking Beasts of Narnia have not forgotten with whom their loyalty lies. Under the cover of darkness, a Rabbit and a few Mice and Moles bring Tirian food and drink and wash his bloodied face (*The Last Battle*, chapter 4).

⊰ HOT CHOCOLATE, WINE, AND CHEESE ⊱

Serve the oatcakes with cheese, such as sharp Cheddar or green cheese, or even spread with a soft cheese like cream cheese or mascarpone. Children can enjoy their meals with mugs of hot chocolate, and grown-ups can have wine.

⊰ OATCAKES WITH FRESH BUTTER ⊱

Use the Oaten Meal Cakes recipe from the "Prince Caspian with His Subjects" menu on page 134. Serve them warm and slathered with butter. A dab of jam won't go amiss either.

Dismal Dinner in the Tower

· Biscuit Porridge ·

After Tirian, Jill, Eustace, and the rest of the Narnians in their company disguise themselves as Calormenes, they turn to the business of getting dinner. Unfortunately, they have nothing but a few hard biscuits, which they pound up and mix with water to make a biscuit porridge. They wish they at least had something soothing to drink with it (*The Last Battle*, chapter 6).

···❧〔 BISCUIT PORRIDGE 🥄🥄🥄 〕❧···

I have to admit, this recipe was a challenge. Biscuit porridge? Ugh! Then I remembered that in the UK, *biscuit* means "cookie," so I took inspiration from that to create this delicious dessert, a far cry from the dismal dinner our beloved Narnians suffered.

CHOCOLATE-CHIP BISCUITS

3½ cups all-purpose flour

½ teaspoon salt

1 teaspoon baking soda

16 tablespoons (1 cup) butter, melted and cooled

1 cup dark brown sugar

½ cup granulated sugar

2 large eggs, at room temperature

2 teaspoons pure vanilla extract

2 cups chocolate chips (12-ounce bag)

MILK SAUCE

2 tablespoons butter

2 tablespoons all-purpose flour

1½ cups whole milk

1 teaspoon pure vanilla extract

I. To make the biscuits, preheat the oven to 375°F and line 2 baking sheets with parchment paper.

2. Whisk together the flour, salt, and baking soda in a large mixing bowl. In a separate bowl, beat the butter, brown sugar, and granulated sugar with a wooden spoon until smooth, about 30 seconds. Add the eggs one at a time, beating after each until incorporated. Add the vanilla and beat until combined.

3. Add the flour mixture and stir to combine. Stir in the chocolate chips. Use a cookie scoop or tablespoon to portion out the dough onto the baking sheets, about 2 inches apart. Bake for 10 minutes, rotating and switching the pans halfway through baking.

   > The cookies will be pale and appear underbaked, but if you bake them any longer, they will get hard. They will stay soft and chewy if you underbake them.

4. To make the milk sauce, melt the butter in a small saucepan. Add the flour, stirring to combine. Pour in the milk and cook, stirring, until smooth. Continue to cook until thick and bubbling, stirring occasionally. Cook about 5 minutes longer to cook out the raw flour taste. Remove from the heat, stir in the vanilla, and strain through a sieve. Discard the solids.

5. To serve, crumble 2 cookies into a dessert bowl. Pour about 2 tablespoons of the milk sauce over the cookies and stir. This porridge is delicious warm or at room temperature.

Makes 3 dozen cookies and about 1¾ cup milk sauce (you will have some cookies left over, but, trust me, that will not be a problem)

Chapter Four
FABULOUS FEASTS

In The Chronicles of Narnia, C. S. Lewis describes feasts much like the ancient medieval great-hall-in-the-castle feasts, with a curious mixture of dishes both ancient and modern, like roasted sides of meat and ices. Ices are ancient, to be sure, but they weren't served in the great halls of the Anglo-Norman kings.

As in Narnia, the typical medieval feast was accompanied by entertainment, drinking, and revelry. The expression "food fit for a king" had special poignancy in those days; the king and the nobility dined on exquisitely sophisticated fare even by today's standards, while the masses starved and died in vast numbers. Historians describe the desperation that led some to eat sheep dung and even their own children. It's hard to imagine how the royal family and the aristocracy could have been so indifferent to their subjects, but nevertheless, they were. Utterly absorbed in fighting their territorial battles and indulging their passion for good food, entertainment, and socializing in between battles, they gave little or no thought to the plight of the poor.

Having said that, it's truly astonishing to discover just how advanced cuisine was for the nobility in those days. An ancient cookbook from the time period describes in great detail how to color food and what shapes to serve it in (to make it look like a rose, for example, or a castle with crenellations). The people who lived during this time and who could afford it took great delight in well-presented food and subtle and complex flavors. The accepted notion that they spiced food heavily to disguise rotting meat is a myth. So is the idea of a bunch of debauched Viking-like knights eating with their fingers while sauce and grease dripped into their beards and onto their clothes. Food historian Colin Spencer argues that these people were so meticulous about their clothes (the ruffs had to be a certain size), their hair (it had to be curled just so), their shoes (perfectly pointy), and their manners (which they called courtly behavior), that it's impossible to imagine them rolling around at the table getting food in their beards and on their clothes.

There was protocol to be followed at the feast, too. The high raised table was for the king, his family, and his favorites. The lower tables were designated by rank; the ranks of the guests dropped as the seating moved closer to the end of the great hall. The courses also followed a specific routine: first came the pottages, then the meat dishes, then the egg and fish dishes, then the pies and pasties (which were often small and meant to be eaten as finger food), then the fried dishes, then the small game birds together with sweet dishes, and finally the spiced wine and comfits.

A new form of entertainment accompanied every course. There were singers, jesters, and great pies with removable lids that, when cut open, released live birds, frogs, and even dwarves (which explains the famous line in the nursery rhyme, "When the pie was opened, the birds began to sing."). The exciting moment that drew gasps of admiration was when a treat called a *subtlety* was brought forth. This was a huge creation of art made of *marchpane*, the old-fashioned word for marzipan, a soft confection made from almonds that can be rolled or shaped and colored to look like fruit or other things. With their knowledge of how to color food, the king's cooks would create a complete three-dimensional scene of, for example, a castle, complete with a moat and peacocks. These were feasts truly fit for a king.

Night Feast at Cair Paravel

First Course
· Pottage of Cabbage and Leeks · Fried Spinach ·

Second Course
· Mawmenee · Bukkenade ·

Third Course
· Caudle Ferry · Pynnonade · Caudle of Salmon ·

Fourth Course
· Veal Pasties · Onion Tarts ·

Fifth Course
· Cryspels (Fried Dough) · Breaded Fried Veal Chops ·

Sixth Course
· Small Game Birds · Apple Fritters · Darioles ·
· Poached Pears in Wine · Nut and Fruit Cake ·

SEVENTH COURSE

· Hot Spiced Wine or Cider · Comfits ·

After the Pevensies are crowned and sceptered, the Narnians enjoy "a great feast" complete with "revelry and dancing." Usually, C. S. Lewis lists the dishes served at these occasions, but in this case, he leaves it up to our imaginations. In keeping with the theme of medieval fantasy, I've re-created a typical medieval feast.

To re-create this medieval feast, I drew inspiration from *The Forme of Cury*, a cookbook from circa 1390 compiled by the master cooks of King Richard II. Its title means "the proper method of cooking." Nearly every recipe in the following feast is drawn directly from this book. My ability to decipher Middle English is now much improved, and I got a kick out of such instructions as to "smite" your chicken in half, "hew" it into small pieces, "hack" it into "gobbets," and "cast" it into a pot. You can almost picture these cooks wearing armor rather than chef's aprons to do battle with their food.

Although I tried to be as authentic as possible, I turned to modern implements such as a food processor instead of a mortar and pestle for grinding or pounding, a sieve instead of a cloth for straining liquids, and a candy thermometer instead of testing sugar syrup by dropping the syrup into cold water to determine what stage it has reached. I also strayed from the beaten path where common sense dictated or when my palate objected.

The structure of the courses is based on the menu written by food historian Colin Spencer in his history on British food, which is listed in the introduction to this chapter. Because many dishes were included in each course, I've chosen two for each as a sample—except for the dessert course, because to me that's the best part of the meal.

One more word: Medieval cooks used saffron often as much for its bright yellow color as to impart flavor to the finished dish. Although I've included it in the following recipes for authenticity's sake, I have made it an optional ingredient due to its high price.

First Course

·⊰[Pottage of Cabbage and Leeks 🥄🥄🥄]⊱·

The nobles and peasants both ate pottage, but while they used the same word, it meant something wholly different to each group. The peasants' pottage was coarse and hearty, filled with peas and beans and any vegetables and herbs they could find, while the nobles' was more delicate, consisting of one or two vegetables that were pounded and sieved to produce a smooth and vibrantly colored soup.

2 tablespoons vegetable oil
1 onion, chopped
1 bunch leeks, chopped
1 cup shredded cabbage

1½ quarts (6 cups) chicken broth
1 bay leaf
Salt, to taste
Freshly ground black pepper, to taste

1. Heat the oil in a large pot. Add the onion and leeks and cook over medium-high heat, stirring occasionally, until the vegetables soften and are just starting to brown, about 15 minutes. Add the cabbage, broth, and bay leaf. Bring to a simmer and cook over low heat until the vegetables are completely soft, 1 to 1½ hours.

2. Remove from the heat. Taste and adjust the seasonings with salt and pepper.

Serves 8

> To make a pounded and sieved soup, puree the soup in batches in a blender or food processor, or use an immersion blender to puree the soup in the pot. Place a sieve over a large bowl and pour the soup, in batches, through the sieve, pushing down with a rubber spatula to extract as much liquid as possible. Return the now thin broth to the pot and reheat. This process will take some time, will be somewhat tedious, and will reduce the amount of soup to about 6 servings.

·⊰[Fried Spinach 🥄🥄🥄]⊱·

1 pound frozen spinach
2 tablespoons vegetable oil

½ teaspoon salt
¼ teaspoon freshly ground pepper

1. Microwave the spinach in a large microwave-safe bowl, uncovered, for 10 to 15 minutes, stirring every 5 minutes, until hot through and through. (Using frozen spinach in this way saves you the hassle of cooking fresh spinach and squeezing out the water.)

2. Heat the oil in a large skillet. Combine the spinach with the salt and pepper and spread in an even layer on the skillet. Cook over medium-high heat until the spinach turns dark on the bottom, about 5 minutes, then carefully turn the spinach, in portions, with a spatula and cook another 5 minutes.

Serves 4

Second Course

·⊷⟨ mawmenee 🥄🥄🥄 ⟩⊶·

This stew is spelled several different ways throughout *The Forme of Cury*.
Sweet and sour was a popular flavor profile in those times, and you'll
find that this stew and the bukkenade that follows fit that description.
This type of dish can be served, as the medievals had it, over slices of
toasted bread called trenchers, or over rice.

1 pound boneless, skinless chicken
    breast, cut into 1-inch cubes
½ cup all-purpose flour
3 tablespoons vegetable oil, divided
¼ cup chopped dates
2 tablespoons pine nuts
1 cup dry white wine
1 cup chicken broth

½ teaspoon salt
⅛ teaspoon ground cloves
⅛ teaspoon ground cinnamon
⅛ teaspoon ground ginger
1 tablespoon sugar
Slices of toasted bread or cooked rice,
    for serving

1. In a large mixing bowl, toss the chicken with the flour. Dust off the excess flour
   and discard. Heat 2 tablespoons oil in a large skillet. Add the chicken pieces
   and cook over medium-high heat, tossing and stirring, until the chicken is
   no longer pink inside, 3 to 5 minutes. Transfer the chicken to a large plate
   or bowl.

2. Add the remaining tablespoon of oil to the skillet. Add the dates and pine nuts
   and fry over medium-high heat until the pine nuts begin to brown, about 2
   minutes. Add the wine, broth, salt, cloves, cinnamon, ginger, and sugar and
   stir to combine. Add the chicken pieces to the skillet and cook and stir until the
   mixture thickens. Simmer, covered, for 10 minutes.

3. Serve over slices of toasted bread or rice.

Serves 4

⋅≈[Bukkenade ♪ ♪ ♪]≈⋅

This sweet-and-sour veal stew is thickened with ground almonds.

1 pound veal, cut into 1-inch cubes
1 tablespoon vegetable oil
1 onion, chopped
2 tablespoons chopped fresh parsley
1 tablespoon chopped fresh sage
½ teaspoon salt
½ teaspoon freshly ground black pepper
½ cup dry white wine

1½ cups chicken broth
½ cup whole raw almonds, finely ground
½ cup currants or dark raisins
2 teaspoons brown sugar
¼ teaspoon ground ginger
Slices of toasted bread or cooked rice, for serving

1. Spray a Dutch oven or wide pot with cooking spray and sear the veal cubes over high heat until crusty brown on 2 sides, 3 to 4 minutes per side. Transfer to a large plate.

2. Reduce the heat to medium. Add the oil, onion, parsley, sage, salt, and pepper. Stir, scraping up the browned bits on the bottom of the pot, and cook until the onion softens and the bottom of the pot darkens, about 7 minutes. Add the wine, broth, almonds, raisins, brown sugar, and ginger and stir to combine. Add the veal along with any accumulated juices.

3. Bring the stew to a simmer and cook 1½ to 2 hours, until the veal is tender. Stir occasionally, checking to make sure the stew doesn't dry out. If it thickens too much, add a little water to thin it out.

4. Serve over slices of toasted bread or rice.

Serves 4

THIRD COURSE

·≍] CAUDLE FERRY ⸗ ≍·

The original caudle is a hot, sweetened, and spiced drink of ale or wine thickened with egg yolks. During the Middle Ages, an eating caudle called caudle ferry, which was further thickened with breadcrumbs, was popular. This dish is much like a pudding.

I found the all-wine version of the caudle ferry inedible, so I tried substituting almond milk for some of the wine, because that was a popular milk substitute back in the day. That would have still made it possible to eat on fast days, when people abstained from meat and dairy products. But in the end, the only way to make this taste good was to use cow's milk. Because the wine doesn't get much cooking time, this recipe is for the grown-ups.

3 cups (4 ounces) fresh breadcrumbs
½ cup dry white wine
1 cup whole milk
¼ cup sugar
⅛ teaspoon salt

Pinch saffron, optional
3 large egg yolks
1 tablespoon sugar mixed with
    1 teaspoon ground ginger, for
    sprinkling

1. Combine the breadcrumbs, wine, milk, sugar, salt, and saffron, if using, in a small saucepan and bring to a boil. Whisk ½ cup of the hot mixture into the egg yolks. Pour the egg yolk mixture into the pan and cook over medium heat, stirring constantly, until the mixture thickens and is bubbling slightly, about 5 minutes.

2. Divide the caudle into 4 saucers and sprinkle with the ginger sugar.

Serves 4

·⟩[PYNNONADE ♩♩♩]⟨·

This delicately flavored almond and pine nut pudding is as enjoyable today as it was over six centuries ago. The name derives from the pine nuts in this dish.

1 tablespoon vegetable oil	*¼ teaspoon ground cinnamon*
½ cup pine nuts	*¼ teaspoon ground ginger*
½ cup blanched almonds (see sidebar)	*2 large egg yolks*
1½ cups almond milk	*1 tablespoon cornstarch*
¼ cup sugar	*Pinch salt*

1. Heat the oil in a small saucepan. Add the pine nuts and cook over medium-high heat, stirring constantly, until golden, 1 or 2 minutes. (The pine nuts burn very easily, so take care not to overcook.) Drain on paper towels.

> To blanch almonds, put them in a bowl and pour boiling water over them. Let them steep for 2 minutes, and then the skins will slip right off. If the skins are still hard to remove, leave them in the water a few minutes longer.

2. Place the blanched almonds in a food processor and process to fine crumbs. Add the almond milk and process until smooth. Pour the mixture into a small saucepan and add the sugar, salt, cinnamon, and ginger. Cook, stirring frequently, until hot but not bubbling. In the meantime, whisk the egg yolks with the cornstarch. Pour ½ cup of the hot mixture into the yolks while whisking constantly. Then pour the yolk mixture into the pan and cook over medium heat, stirring constantly, until the mixture is thick and bubbling.

3. Remove the pan from the heat, stir in the pine nuts, and divide among 4 dessert bowls or saucers. Allow to cool slightly before serving or serve at room temperature.

Serves 4

·⊰[CAUDLE OF SALMON ♪♪♪]⊱·

This was an important recipe for a fish day, a day when no milk or meat could be eaten. The Church established fish days, or fast days, such as Lent and Advent as well as Wednesdays and Fridays, to prevent gluttony. The Church also believed—as it does to this day—that fasting makes it easier to commune with God. This salmon recipe calls for almond milk, which made it acceptable to eat on a fish day. Almond milk was used a lot for this reason.

1½ pounds salmon fillet, skinned, cut into ½-inch pieces

1 cup water

1 tablespoon vegetable oil

4 ounces (about 1 cup) chopped whites of leeks, or 1 onion, chopped (the leeks give a milder flavor)

1 ounce (about 1 cup or 2 slices) torn white bread

1 cup almond milk

¾ teaspoon salt

½ teaspoon freshly ground black pepper

Pinch ground mace

Pinch ground cloves

Pinch ground ginger

2 pinches saffron, optional

1. Simmer the salmon in the water in a medium pot until cooked through, about 15 minutes. Meanwhile, heat the oil in a medium or large saucepan and add the leeks. Sauté over medium heat until the leeks begin to brown, stirring frequently, about 10 minutes.

2. While the leeks are cooking, remove the salmon with a slotted spoon to a large plate. Strain the cooking liquid and measure out 1¼ cups (add water if there isn't enough cooking liquid). Process the bread and almond milk in a blender or food processor until smooth. Pour the cooking liquid into the leeks. Add the salt, pepper, mace, cloves, ginger, and saffron, if using.

3. Add the almond milk and bread mixture to the leek mixture and cook until thick and bubbling. Turn off the heat, add the salmon, and stir to combine.

Serves 4

FOURTH COURSE

⋅∘[veal pasties 𝄢𝄢𝄢]∘⋅

When I saw this recipe in *The Forme of Cury*, all I could think was "ugh." This is the classic ancient mincemeat pie, which was made with real minced meat, dried fruit, and sweet spices. Today, the meat is left out of mincemeat pie because it doesn't suit the modern palate. Because most of us prefer not to mix our entrées with our desserts, I left out the fruit and sugar and kept only a tiny hint of the sweet spices, changing the "ugh" to "yum."

PASTY DOUGH

2½ cups all-purpose flour

1 teaspoon salt

16 tablespoons (1 cup) butter or margarine, chilled and cubed

½ to ¾ cup ice water, as needed

VEAL FILLING

1 pound veal stew cubes

1 cup chicken broth

2 tablespoons oil

1 onion, chopped

1 teaspoon all-purpose flour

2 large hard-boiled eggs

½ teaspoon salt

¼ teaspoon freshly ground black pepper

⅛ teaspoon ground cinnamon

⅛ teaspoon ground ginger

1. To make the pie dough, place the flour and salt in a food processor and pulse to combine. Scatter the butter pieces over the flour-salt mixture and give a few quick pulses until the mixture forms a coarse yellow meal. Turn the mixture into a large mixing bowl, sprinkle ½ cup water on top, and fold with a rubber spatula until the dough comes together. If the dough is too dry, add more water 1 tablespoon at a time. Divide the dough in half, form into disks, wrap in plastic wrap, and refrigerate at least 30 minutes or up to 2 days.

> You can use frozen pre-rolled puff pastry dough cut into 5-inch squares to save time.

2. To make the filling, simmer the veal cubes in the broth in a medium pot for 2 hours. Drain the veal, reserving the cooking liquid, and cool the veal. Refrigerate the veal until cold or until needed, up to 3 days. If not using immediately, refrigerate the cooking liquid as well, up to 3 days.

3. Heat the oil in a medium skillet and add the onion. Cook over medium-high heat, stirring often, until brown, about 15 minutes. Add the flour and stir to combine. Add ¼ cup of the cooking liquid from the veal and cook until the mixture turns thick and bubbly, about 5 minutes.

4. Place the veal and eggs in a food processor and pulse until finely chopped. Turn the mixture into a large mixing bowl and add the onion mixture, salt, and spices. Mix well.

5. Preheat the oven to 425°F and line a baking sheet with parchment paper. Working with 1 disk of dough at a time, roll out the dough on a floured work surface ⅛ inch thick. Use a saucer to cut out 6-inch circles of dough (you should get 6 to 7 circles with a lot of leftover dough scraps; discard the scraps). Divide the filling among the dough circles, moisten the edges with water, fold over, and crimp with your fingers or a fork to seal. Cut slits for vents. Place the pasties on the baking sheet and bake for 25 to 30 minutes, rotating halfway through baking, until golden.

Makes 6 to 7 pasties

··ᢀ[onion tarts 🥄🥄🥄]ᢁ··

King Richard II's cooks really knew their stuff: these little tarts are delicious.

Tart Dough
¼ cup all-purpose flour
½ teaspoon salt

8 tablespoons (½ cup) butter, chilled and cubed
4 to 6 tablespoons ice water

Onion Filling
2 tablespoons butter
1 onion, chopped

¾ cup whole milk
1 large egg

½ ounce white bread, no crusts
(about 1 slice)

½ teaspoon salt

¼ teaspoon freshly ground black
pepper

⅛ teaspoon ground ginger

½ teaspoon sugar

1. To make the tart dough, place the flour and salt in a food processor and pulse
   to combine. Scatter the butter pieces over the dough and give a few quick pulses
   until the mixture forms a coarse yellow meal. Turn the mixture into a
   large mixing bowl, sprinkle 4 tablespoons water on top, and fold with a
   rubber spatula until the dough comes together. If the dough is too dry,
   add more water 1 tablespoon at a time. Form the dough into a disk,
   wrap in plastic wrap, and refrigerate at least 30 minutes or up to 2 days.

   > You can use frozen pie dough to save time.

2. To make the filling, heat the butter in a medium pan and add the onion. Cook
   over medium heat, stirring frequently, until the onion is well browned. Set
   aside to cool. Put the remaining filling ingredients into a food processor or
   blender and process until smooth. Transfer the mixture to a mixing bowl and
   stir in the onion.

3. Preheat the oven to 350°F. Roll out the dough on a floured work surface ⅛–
   inch thick. Cut out 4¼–inch circles and fit them into the cups of a 6-cup muffin pan. Divide the filling among the shells (you will have some leftover filling)
   and bake for 35 minutes, until the tops are puffed and the crust is pale golden.

Makes 6 tarts

FIFTH COURSE

·∘] CRYSPELS (FRIED DOUGH) 🥄🥄🥄 [∘·

When I tested this recipe, I did not expect these bits of dough to puff up. They're like very small doughnuts, and they're delicious enough to eat on their own, without the recommended honey and custard.

DOUGH

1¼ cups all-purpose flour
1 tablespoon sugar
½ teaspoon salt

8 tablespoons (½ cup) butter, chilled
 and cubed
4 to 6 tablespoons ice water

CUSTARD

1½ cups whole milk
¼ cup sugar
1 tablespoon cornstarch
3 large egg yolks, beaten

1 teaspoon pure vanilla extract
Vegetable oil, for frying
Honey, for serving

1. To make the pie dough, place the flour, sugar, and salt in a food processor and pulse to combine. Scatter the butter pieces over the dough and give a few quick pulses until the mixture forms a coarse yellow meal. Turn the mixture into a large mixing bowl, sprinkle 4 tablespoons water on top, and fold with a rubber spatula until the dough comes together. If the dough is too dry, add more water 1 tablespoon at a time. Form the dough into a disk, wrap in plastic wrap, and refrigerate at least 30 minutes or up to 2 days.

2. To make the custard, combine the milk, sugar, and cornstarch in a medium saucepan. Cook over medium heat, stirring constantly, just until the mixture turns hot, but not bubbling, about 5 minutes. Whisk ½ cup of the hot mixture into the egg yolks. Pour the egg yolk mixture into the pan and cook, stirring constantly, until the mixture is thick and bubbling, about 5 minutes. Remove from the heat and stir in the vanilla extract. Strain the custard through a fine-mesh sieve into a bowl, cover with plastic wrap, and leave at room temperature

until ready to use (refrigerate if not using within a few hours, up to 1 week; then gently rewarm in a microwave).

3. Fill a saucepan about 1 or 2 inches with oil. Clip a thermometer to the side of the pot and heat to 350°F. While the oil is heating, roll out the dough on a floured surface ⅛–inch thick and cut out 2½–inch circles. Fry the cryspels in batches until pale golden, 1 to 2 minutes per side (the cryspels will float to the top of the oil after a few seconds). Maintain the oil at a temperature of 350°F to 370°F. Drain the fried cryspels on paper towels. Do not reroll the scraps of dough, but you can cut them up and fry them as well.

To check if the oil is hot enough without a thermometer, drop a piece of bread into the oil. It should bubble up immediately but not turn brown right away.

4. To serve, place 2 tablespoons custard on a dessert plate. Pile 6 cryspels over the custard and drizzle honey on the top.

Serves 4, with extra scraps

·⇥[Breaded Fried Veal Chops ❘❘❘]⇤·

THANKS TO MOM FOR THIS RECIPE.

I was very excited to see this in *The Forme of Cury* because as a kid, I had it every year for one of the holidays. I remember looking forward to this dish every year.

Vegetable oil, for frying
4 veal chops
2 large eggs, beaten

Seasoned breadcrumbs, for coating,
or breadcrumbs seasoned with
salt, pepper, and dried parsley

1. Fill a skillet with ¼ inch oil and heat over medium-high heat until the oil bubbles when you dip in a veal chop. Dip the veal chops in the beaten eggs, then coat with the breadcrumbs. Fry until golden brown, 4 to 5 minutes per side.

Serves 4

Sixth Course

·⊰[Small Game Birds]⊱·

For these dishes, use the recipe for pigeon stew from the "Poggin the Dwarf Makes Breakfast" menu on page 30 and the recipe for stuffed snipe from the "Shasta's Dinner as Corin" menu on page 125. That will provide your course of small game birds to give an authentic feel to your medieval feast.

·⊰[Apple Fritters 🥄🥄🥄]⊱·

3 large sweet apples, such as Gala, peeled, cored, and sliced into ½-inch thick rings
5 tablespoons sugar, divided
1 large egg
⅓ cup ale
⅔ cup whole milk
Pinch saffron, optional
1 cup all-purpose flour
⅛ teaspoon salt
Vegetable oil, for frying
1 tablespoon sugar mixed with 1 teaspoon ground cinnamon, for sprinkling

1. Toss the apples with 2 tablespoons of the sugar and cook over medium heat in a covered medium pot, stirring occasionally, until the apples are slightly softened and the juices are released, about 15 minutes. Drain the apples and set aside to cool.

2. In a large mixing bowl, whisk together the egg, ale, milk, and saffron, if using. In a separate bowl, whisk together the flour, salt, and remaining sugar until smooth. Add the flour mixture to the egg mixture and whisk just until moistened; the batter will be thick and lumpy. Fill a large skillet with ¼ inch oil and heat the oil. Dip the apple rings in the batter to coat, then shake off the excess batter. Fry the fritters until golden brown, about 3 minutes per side. Drain on paper towels.

3. Serve about 3 fritters per person. Sprinkle the cinnamon sugar on top.

Makes about 4 servings

·⊰[DARIOLES ♪♪♪]⊱·

Dariole is an old-fashioned word for a small custard pie. I tried making the custard using the spices of the time, but I guess I just really like plain old vanilla, which wasn't introduced to Europe until about 130 years after *The Forme of Cury* was written.

PASTRY DOUGH

1¼ cups all-purpose flour

1 tablespoon sugar

½ teaspoon salt

8 tablespoons (½ cup) butter, chilled and cubed

4 to 6 tablespoons ice water

CUSTARD FILLING

½ cup whole milk

¼ cup heavy cream

⅛ teaspoon salt

1 tablespoon sugar

Pinch saffron, optional

1 large egg yolk

1 teaspoon cornstarch

1 teaspoon vanilla

1. To make the pie dough, place the flour, sugar, and salt in a food processor and pulse to combine. Scatter the butter pieces over the flour mixture and give a few quick pulses until the mixture forms a coarse yellow meal. Turn the mixture into a large mixing bowl, sprinkle 4 tablespoons water on top, and fold with a rubber spatula until the dough comes together. If the dough is too dry, add more water 1 tablespoon at a time. Form the dough into a disk, wrap in plastic wrap, and refrigerate at least 30 minutes or up to 2 days.

> You can use frozen pie dough to save time.

2. Preheat the oven to 425°F. Roll out the dough on a floured work surface ⅛-inch thick and cut out 4½-inch circles. Fit the circles into the cups of a 6-cup muffin tin and flute the edges, if desired. Prick the dough all over with a fork and freeze for 10 minutes. Fit a piece of aluminum foil into each pastry shell and fill with pie weights or beans. Bake for 30 minutes.

3. While the shells are prebaking, combine the milk, heavy cream, salt, sugar, and saffron, if using, in a small saucepan and cook over medium-high heat, stirring, until the salt, sugar, and saffron are dissolved and the mixture is hot. Whisk the

egg yolk with the cornstarch. Whisk ½ cup of the milk mixture into the egg yolks, then pour the yolk mixture into the pan while whisking constantly, just until hot. Turn off the heat (the custard does not need to be fully cooked). Stir in the vanilla and strain the custard into a 2-cup measuring cup with a spout for easy pouring.

4. Remove the pan from the oven, reduce the heat to 350°F, remove the foil and weights, and fill the shells with the custard. Return the darioles to the oven and cook for 15 minutes, until the custard is puffed up.

5. The custard will fall as it cools. Cool to room temperature before serving.

Makes 6 darioles

···⊰[POACHED PEARS IN WINE 🥄🥄🥄]⊱···

Who knew this classic recipe was so old?

4 firm pears, such as Bartlett   *1 cup sugar*
3 cups dry red wine   *1 teaspoon ground ginger*

1. Peel, halve, and core the pears. Bring the wine to a simmer in a wide saucepan and place the pears in the wine. Simmer, covered, until the pears are easily pierced with a fork, about 30 minutes, turning them over several times. Drain the pears and return the wine to the saucepan. Cover the pears to keep them from drying out.

2. Add the sugar and ginger to the wine and boil, uncovered, until the wine is reduced by about half, about 15 minutes. Lay the pears in the syrup and cook 10 minutes more, turning the pears over once or twice. Remove from the heat and cool to room temperature. Serve the pears in bowls and pour the syrup over each serving. Serve warm, at room temperature, or chilled.

Serves 4

···⊰[NUT AND FRUIT CAKE 🥄🥄🥄]⊱···

This is the only recipe in this feast that I did not take from *The Forme of Cury*. Instead, I drew my inspiration from food historians Alan Davidson's and Colin Spencer's descriptions of rich breads from the

Middle Ages. Spencer draws a comparison between such a type of bread and panforte, an Italian nut and fruit cake dating back to the 1200s, so I took a look at panforte recipes as well before creating my own. This cake is like a chewy candy bar, so if you're not a fan of the traditional Christmas fruitcake, consider substituting this one.

1 cup sugar

½ cup honey

½ cup heavy cream

¼ teaspoon salt

1 cup whole almonds

½ cup walnut pieces

½ cup golden raisins

½ cup chopped dates

½ cup chopped figs

½ cup all-purpose flour

1 teaspoon ground cinnamon

¼ teaspoon ground ginger

⅛ teaspoon ground cloves

⅛ teaspoon ground mace

1 large egg, beaten

1. Preheat the oven to 325°F. Spray a 9-inch round cake pan with baking spray with flour and line the bottom and sides with parchment paper. Greasing the pan first helps the paper stick. Do not skip lining both the bottom and the sides of the pan so you will be able to easily remove the cake from the pan. Combine the sugar, honey, heavy cream, and salt in a medium saucepan. Cook over medium-high heat, stirring constantly, until the sugar is dissolved and the mixture is bubbling. Wash down the sides of the pot with a pastry brush dipped in hot water and clip a candy thermometer to the side of the pot. Cook, stirring constantly, over medium-high heat, until the mixture reaches 238°F. Remove the pan from the heat and cool to below 150°F.

2. While the sugar syrup is cooling, combine the nuts and dried fruit in a large mixing bowl. In a separate bowl, whisk together the flour and spices, then pour the flour mixture over the nut-fruit mixture and toss to combine. Add the egg to the cooled sugar syrup (make sure the syrup has cooled properly first—if it is too hot, the egg will cook) and mix well. Add the sugar syrup mixture to the nut-fruit mixture and stir to combine. Scrape the batter into the prepared pan.

3. Bake for 1 hour, until the cake is puffed and golden. Cool completely before inverting onto a plate. Leave the parchment paper on and invert again. It will be easier to remove slices with the parchment paper on. Use a sharp chef's knife to slice this cake.

Makes 16 servings

Seventh Course

···ᵉ][HOT SPICED WINE OR CIDER]ᵉ···

Use the recipe for spiced wine (or mulled cider for the kids) from the "Snack on the Ship in the Picture" menu on page 69. The spiced wine provides a pleasant finish to this elaborate feast.

···ᵉ][COMFITS]ᵉ···

Use the recipe for comfits from the "Snack Suggested by a Giantess" menu on page 77. At such a feast, guests would take the spiced wine and comfits standing, as the servants at this point had cleared away and moved the tables.

Celebration Feast in Cair Paravel

· Sides of Roasted Meat · Wheaten Cakes · Oaten Meal Cakes ·

· Honey, Many–Colored Sugars, and Cream ·

The Narnians are victorious once again, and in celebration, Bacchus, the wine god (Dionysus in Greek mythology), the Maenads (his followers), and Silenus (his tutor), perform a magical dance that produces a feast (*Prince Caspian*, chapter 15).

·⊰[SIDES OF ROASTED MEAT]⊱·

"Sides of roasted meat" refers to the whole side of an animal; it's a lot of meat for a dinner party! But it was probably enough to feed the hordes of Narnians who were with Aslan. Use the recipe for Braised Beef on page 91.

·⊰[WHEATEN CAKES]⊱·

Many centuries ago, what we call cakes today meant something else: a round, flat bread type of thing, often cooked on something like a griddle. The Egyptians sweetened these types of round cakes with honey, and the Romans added ingredients like dried fruit and wine—and even used yeast, which would make the product a sort of rich bread. In the Middle Ages, fats like cream and butter were added, as well as eggs, making for an even richer yeasted cake. This recipe uses baking powder, though, which is of course a lot faster to make and yields a more tender rather than chewy crumb.

1 cup all-purpose flour

½ cup white whole-wheat flour (see sidebar)

1 teaspoon ground cinnamon

1½ teaspoons baking powder

½ teaspoon baking soda

¼ teaspoon salt

8 tablespoons (½ cup) butter, at room temperature

1 cup sugar

2 large eggs, at room temperature

½ cup buttermilk, at room temperature

1. Adjust the oven rack to the middle position and preheat the oven to 350°F. Line a 12-cup muffin pan with cupcake liners or spray the pan with baking spray with flour.

2. In a large mixing bowl, whisk together the flours, cinnamon, baking powder, baking soda, and salt.

3. In a separate bowl, beat the butter and sugar until light and fluffy, scraping down the sides as necessary, about 5 minutes. Add the eggs one at time, beating after each until incorporated. Add the flour mixture and buttermilk alternately, mixing on the slowest speed, starting and finishing with the flour. Give the batter a final stir with a rubber spatula.

> You can find white whole-wheat flour in the baking aisle. I prefer it to regular whole-wheat for its lighter color and texture, though it contains the same nutrients as regular whole wheat.

4. Divide the batter into the pan using a spring-loaded ice cream scoop or use a tablespoon to divide the batter among the 12 cups. Bake for 25 minutes, until firm to the touch, rotating the pan halfway through baking. The tops will be pale but golden around the edges.

Makes 12 cakes

·❦[OATEN MEAL CAKES]❧·

Use the recipe for Oaten Meal Cakes from the "Prince Caspian with His Subjects" menu on page 134. People have been eating oaten meal cakes for centuries, so it's not surprising that the feast at Cair Paravel included these hearty treats.

⊰⟦ Honey, Many-Colored Sugars, and Cream ⟧⊱

Serve this meal with pitchers of honey and cream, which are delicious with the Oaten Meal Cakes. You can find colored sugars in the cake decorating aisle of your grocery store. You can sprinkle these on your oaten meal cakes or stir into your milk to make fun colors.

THE FEAST OF THE THREE SLEEPERS

· Roast Turkey · Roast Goose · Peacocks · Roasted Stuffed Boar's Head ·
· Sides of Venison · Pies in the Shape of Ships, Dragons, and Elephants ·
· Ice Puddings (Nesselrode Pudding · Frozen Lemon Posset) ·
· Cornish Buttered Lobster · Salmon with Butter and Herbs · Nuts ·
· Grapes, Pineapple, Peaches, Pomegranates, Melons ·
· Oven–Roasted Tomato Medley ·

"Don't touch the food" is the first thought the travelers on the *Dawn Treader* think after they disembark on an island and find a table laden with the dishes described in this menu section—and three men in an obviously enchanted sleep sitting at the table. But soon, the star daughter appears and assures them the food is safe to eat, and they fall to it with gusto (*The Voyage of the Dawn Treader*, chapter 13).

ROAST TURKEY

Because turkey breasts and thighs cook at different rates, turkey experts offer different types of culinary gymnastics to get the breasts and thighs to be done at the same time. The easiest method I've learned is to start with a high temperature and then reduce it, and to flip the bird midway through cooking.

1 (12- to 14-pound) turkey
Olive oil, for smearing
Salt, for sprinkling

Freshly ground black pepper, for sprinkling
2 cups water

1.   Preheat the oven to 400°F. Place the turkey breast-side down (upside down)

on the V-rack of a large roasting pan. Smear with olive oil and sprinkle evenly with the salt and pepper. Pour the water into the pan.

2. Roast for 1 hour, rotating the pan after 30 minutes. Remove the roasting pan from the oven and flip the bird breast side up (right side up) using silicone oven mitts, kitchen towels, or thick wads of paper towels. Brush the top with olive oil and sprinkle evenly with salt and pepper.

> To make a good gravy, before putting the roasting pan in the oven, scatter 2 carrots, cut into chunks; 2 celery ribs, cut into chunks; 1 sliced onion; and about a half head of garlic, cloves peeled, on the bottom of the pan. When the turkey is done, pour the drippings into a fat separator, and measure ½ cup. Or you can pour the drippings into a container, wait about 10 minutes for the fat to rise to the top, and then skim off the fat. In a small saucepan, mix 1 tablespoon flour with 1 tablespoon vegetable oil, cooking over medium heat until smooth. Add 1½ cups chicken broth and the ½ cup drippings, stirring constantly over medium-high heat until the mixture is smooth, thick, and bubbling. Cook 5 to 7 minutes more to remove the raw starch flavor. Makes 2 cups, more than enough to drench 12 servings of mashed potatoes.

3. Return the turkey to the oven and roast for another 2 to 2½ hours, rotating the pan at regular intervals (i.e., after the first hour and after the second hour if not yet ready, or every 30 minutes), until the breast registers 160°F and the thigh registers 170°F. Tent the turkey with foil and allow to rest for 30 minutes before carving (the turkey will continue to cook due to residual heat, and the juices will redistribute during this resting period).

Serves 12 to 16

ROAST GOOSE

Use the recipe from the "Christmas Dinner from Father Christmas" menu on page 119.

PEACOCKS

Peacocks may have beautiful feathers, but they are not good eatin'! I've never tasted peacock, but I'm told its meat is tough and stringy. For a more succulent entree, use the classic roast turkey recipe from the "Dinner from the Giants" menu on page 163 for this dish.

·◄[ROASTED STUFFED BOAR'S HEAD 🥄🥄🥄]►·

THANKS TO CHEF CHRIS KOCH FOR THIS RECIPE.

The legend goes that a fifteenth-century student at The Queen's College in Oxford was walking through the forest with his nose in a book (he was reading Aristotle), when a wild boar attacked him. Having nothing but his book to defend himself with, he shoved it down the boar's throat, choking it to death. In celebration, that night the boar's head was roasted and served to all. Since then, the Boar's Head Feast has become a tradition, with the roasted head carried in a procession while its bearers sing the "Boar's Head Carol," a fifteenth-century Christmas carol written in a mixture of English and Latin.

1 young boar's or pig's head, intact
5 tablespoons butter
2 cups chopped onions
1 cup chopped celery
1 tablespoon poultry seasoning (such
    as Bell's)
1 tablespoon fresh sage leaves,
    chopped
1 teaspoon sea salt
1 cup dry white wine
1 cup pork or chicken stock
7 cups cooked rice

3 pounds Boston butt roast, cut into
    1-inch cubes
2 pounds pork sausage, casings
    removed
1 pound chopped walnuts
6 cups bread cubes (1 pound white
    bread cut into ½-inch cubes)
Kale or other greens, for serving,
    enough to line the platter for
    garnish
1 (15-ounce) can peach halves,
    apricots, or pineapples

1. To loosen the head skin and to cook the head meat, place the head on a shallow rack in a large pot deep enough to cover 1 inch of the base of the head. Bring the water to a simmer and keep the water simmering at that depth while steaming, covered, 2 to 3 hours.

2. After removing the head from the boiler, cool it for 30 minutes, then refrigerate it until thoroughly chilled. Remove the head from the refrigerator and let it warm enough on the outside so the skin is pliable. Put the head on a large cutting board. With a short, thin knife, make a lengthwise incision from the base of the snout to the base of the neck skin, and from a point 2 inches below

the ears to the base of the neck. Beginning at the end of the incision, gently and carefully—especially around the eyes—cut upward under the skin on both sides to loosen the skin as you go. Continue to release the skin, being careful not to puncture it. Some fat will adhere to the skin; leave it on, as it will render away during the roasting and will help give the final brown and shiny look you want in the finished product. Fold the skin, wrap in plastic, and refrigerate until ready to stuff it.

3. Finely chop the meat from inside the head, including the eyes, tongue, and cheeks.

4. Heat a large, heavy skillet or Dutch oven over medium-high heat. Add the butter and melt it. Add the onions, celery, poultry seasoning, sage, salt, wine, and stock. Bring to a boil. Add the pork butt and sausage. Stir to blend, cover, and simmer for 30 minutes.

5. In a large mixing bowl, mix the rice, nuts, bread cubes, cooked head meat, and meat mixture to create the stuffing for the head. The mixture should be slightly moist but not overly wet. Use additional stock, if needed.

6. Preheat the oven to 350°F. Ensure that the skin is at room temperature or warm enough so it is pliable. Prepare a large roasting pan with a rack. Cover the rack with heavy-duty foil, first lengthwise and then crosswise, allowing long enough pieces to encapsulate the whole head and form a pyramid shape over the top. Neatly cut a lengthwise 5-inch gash through the center of the foil to allow excess fat to drain into the roaster.

7. Place the skin face down on a work surface with the snout facing you. Transfer the stuffing to the inside of the skin and pack loosely. Fold the skin together and sew loose stitches with a trussing needle and kitchen string to allow the stuffing to expand during cooking. Transfer the head, right side up, to the foil, and close the foil over the head, crimping to seal.

8. Bake the head for about 2 hours, or until an internal temperature of 165°F is reached. Line a platter with the kale and place the head on top. Surround the head with the canned fruit and present.

Serves 30

⋅∘⟦ SIDES OF VENISON ⟧∘⋅

Use the recipe from the "Supper for Jill and Eustace at Cair Paravel" menu on page 152 for an impressive addition to this feast.

⋅∘⟦ DRAGON, SHIP, AND ELEPHANT PIES (MINCE PIES) 🥄🥄🥄 ⟧∘⋅

The word *pie* comes from the word *magpie* because early pies contained a collection of various ingredients, in the same way that a magpie's collection comprises various items. For example, the fourteenth-century apple pie recipe in *The Forme of Cury* lists raisins, figs, and pears in addition to apples. Although today's pies focus on one main ingredient with just a few supporting ingredients, this recipe, with its raisins, candied peel, apples, and brandy, truly qualifies as magpie-like.

PIE DOUGH

4 cups all-purpose flour, divided in half

¼ cup sugar, divided in half

1 teaspoon salt, divided in half

1 pound (2 cups) butter, chilled, cut into chunks, and divided in half

1 to 1½ cups ice water

MINCEMEAT FILLING

½ cup raisins

½ cup golden raisins

½ cup mixed candied peel

2 tart apples, such as Granny Smith, peeled and chopped

2 sweet apples, such as Gala, peeled and chopped

Grated zest and juice of 1 lemon

Grated zest and juice of 1 orange

¾ cup apple juice

¼ cup brandy

4 tablespoons (¼ cup) butter

1 cup dark brown sugar

1 teaspoon ground cinnamon

¼ teaspoon ground nutmeg

⅛ teaspoon ground cloves

⅛ teaspoon ground allspice

1. To make the pie dough, place 2 cups flour, 2 tablespoons sugar, and ½ teaspoon salt in a food processor and pulse a few seconds until combined. Scatter

½ pound butter pieces over the flour and pulse until the mixture resembles a coarse yellow meal, about 15 pulses. Turn out the dough into a large mixing bowl, and repeat with the remaining flour, sugar, salt, and butter. Add this to the mixing bowl, sprinkle 1 cup water on top, and fold with a rubber spatula until the dough adheres together. If the dough is dry, add water 1 tablespoon at a time (better too wet than too dry). Divide the dough into 3 portions, shape into disks, wrap in plastic wrap, and chill at least 2 hours or up to 3 days.

Some supermarkets carry mixed candied peel, often with other ingredients like pineapple and cherries, during the holiday season. You can also purchase mixed candied peel online, or buy orange and lemon peels separately, also online, and mix them.

To save time and tedium, you can use frozen prerolled pie or puff pastry dough cut into circles or squares and folded over the filling.

2. To make the filling, put all the mincemeat ingredients into a large saucepan and bring to a boil while stirring. Reduce the heat to a simmer and cook until the mixture is thick and most of the liquid has evaporated, stirring occasionally, about 3 hours. Toward the end of the cooking time, as the mixture gets really thick, stir more frequently to prevent scorching. Cool completely. Transfer to an airtight container and chill thoroughly before use.

3. To assemble the pies, adjust the oven racks to the upper and lower middle positions and preheat the oven to 375°F. Line 2 baking sheets with parchment paper and set aside. Working with one batch of dough at a time, roll out the dough on a floured work surface to ⅛-inch thick. Use a large dragon-shaped cookie cutter or cutout (a piece of paper cut into the shape of a dragon; place it on the dough and cut around it with a sharp knife) to cut 6 to 8 dragon shapes. Place about 1 tablespoon of filling on half the dragons and cover with the remaining dragons. Crimp the edges to seal; you can make ridges along the neck with your fingers. Cut an eyehole and scale shapes to make slits. Repeat with the remaining dough, using ship and elephant cookie cutters or cutouts. You should get 3 to 4 pies of each shape. Place the pies on the prepared baking sheets and bake for 30 minutes, switching and rotating the baking sheets halfway through baking.

Makes about 1 dozen pies

⟶⫶] NESSELRODE PUDDING ♪♪♪ [⫶⟵

Ice pudding is an old-fashioned British term for frozen dessert, and one of the most popular iced puddings of the nineteenth century is Nesselrode pudding, named for a visiting Russian diplomat. This recipe is almost identical to the nineteenth-century chef Jules Gouffé's version, updated for use with an ice cream maker. One of the hallmarks of this chestnut dessert is folding in beaten egg whites or whipped cream (or a combination of both, as in Isabella Beeton's recipe). This recipe omits this step for the sake of a denser ice cream (and simplicity). Because of the high alcohol content, kids should stay away. See the sidebar about modifying this for children.

ICE CREAM

½ cup raisins

½ cup golden raisins

½ cup maraschino liqueur or rum

2 cups whole milk

2 cups heavy cream

1 cup sugar

5 large egg yolks

½ cup unsweetened chestnut puree

CUSTARD SAUCE

1½ cups whole milk

¼ cup sugar

3 large egg yolks

2 tablespoons maraschino liqueur or rum

1. To make the ice cream, soak the raisins in the liqueur for 5 hours or overnight.

2. Combine the milk, cream, and sugar in a large saucepan and cook over low heat until hot but not boiling. Temper the egg yolks by adding 1 cup of the hot milk mixture into the yolks while whisking constantly; then pour the yolk mixture into the pan, stirring constantly over medium heat until the mixture has thickened and is hot and steaming but not bubbling.

To unmold, run hot water briefly around the outside of the mold to melt and loosen the pudding. You can use a 2-quart bowl if you don't have a mold, and simply scoop out the ice cream instead of unmolding and slicing.

To make this recipe for children, omit the liqueur or rum and skip the soaking step. Add ½ teaspoon rum extract along with the chestnut puree. Replace the liqueur or rum in the custard sauce with 1 teaspoon pure vanilla extract.

3.   Stir in the chestnut puree. Pour the mixture through a sieve and cover the surface directly with plastic wrap to prevent a skin from forming. Cool to room temperature and then chill until cold, at least 6 hours or overnight.

4.   Spray a 2-quart mold with baking spray. Drain the raisins well and stir in ¼ cup of the liqueur into the chilled chestnut mixture. Reserve the remaining liqueur. Freeze the chestnut custard in an ice cream maker according to the manufacturer's instructions. Toward the end of the freezing, add the raisins. Scrape into the prepared mold and freeze until firm.

5.   To make the custard sauce, heat the milk and sugar and temper the egg yolks as previously described. Strain the custard and stir in the liqueur. Cool to room temperature and chill.

6.   To serve, unmold the pudding. Cut into slices and serve with the chilled custard.

Serves 10

·⊰[FROZEN LEMON POSSET]⊱·

Use the recipe from the "Snack Suggested by a Giantess" menu on page 77 and freeze it before serving.

·⊰[CORNISH BUTTERED LOBSTER 𝄞𝄞𝄞]⊱·

THANKS TO CHEF CHRIS KOCH FOR THIS RECIPE.

The following is advice from *Apicius*, the only surviving Roman cookbook, on how to prepare lobster:

> The shells of the lobsters or crabs [which are cooked] are broken, the meat extracted from the head and pounded in the mortar with pepper and the best kind of broth. This pulp [is shaped into neat little cakes which are fried] and served up nicely.

Lobster and crab cakes are still made today, and this recipe specifies mincing the meat of the lobster as well.

2 (1½ pound) lobsters, live
1 lemon, cut in half
6 tablespoons butter, divided
¼ cup breadcrumbs
2 tablespoons brandy
¼ cup heavy cream
Salt, to taste

1 pinch ground cayenne pepper
Freshly ground black pepper, to taste
Cucumber twists
1 lemon, sliced into wedges, for
    serving
4 dill sprigs, for serving

1. First, kill the lobsters as described in the sidebar to Lobster Rissoles on page 91. Then cut the lobsters in half lengthwise. Discard the stomach, the dark vein that runs through the body, and the spongy gills from each lobster. Remove the tail meat. Crack open the claws and remove the meat. Scrape the meat from the legs with a skewer. Cut the meat into chunks, and then sprinkle with lemon juice by squeezing over the meat with the cut lemon. Remove and reserve the coral, if present. Remove and reserve the soft pink flesh and liver separately.

> Because of the step requiring igniting brandy, children should not attempt to make this recipe.

2. Scrub the shells and place them on a baking sheet in the oven at the lowest possible setting to warm until the rest of the preparation is complete. Melt 2 tablespoons butter in a small skillet, add the breadcrumbs, and cook over medium heat until browned and crisp, stirring constantly and taking care not to burn the breadcrumbs, about 5 minutes. Melt the remaining butter in a medium saucepan, add the lobster flesh, and gently stir until heated through.

3. Pour the brandy in a ladle, ignite with a long match, and pour, still flaming, over the lobster. When the flames have subsided, transfer the lobster to the warmed shells, using a slotted spoon, and keep warm in the low oven.

4. Pound the liver and pink flesh. Stir into the lobster cooking juices. Add the cream, a little salt and cayenne pepper, and plenty of black pepper. Boil briefly until thickened, then spoon over the lobster.

5. Sprinkle the fried breadcrumbs over the top. Quickly garnish with the reserved coral, if available, cucumber twists, lemon slices, and dill sprigs.

Serves 4

⊰[salmon with butter and herbs ♩♩♩]⊱

In Medieval England, salmon was so plentiful that apprentices revolted against the amount of salmon they were served and demanded that it be served no more than three times a week. This salmon is so good, you'll wonder what they were complaining about.

1½ pounds salmon fillet
2 tablespoons butter, melted
½ teaspoon salt
¼ teaspoon freshly ground black
pepper

2 garlic cloves, minced
½ teaspoon dried tarragon
½ teaspoon dried marjoram
¼ teaspoon dried sage

1. Adjust the oven rack to the middle position and preheat the oven to 425°F.
2. Remove the skin from the salmon and place it, skinned side down, on a greased rimmed baking sheet. Combine the melted butter with the salt, pepper, garlic, and herbs and brush the mixture over the fish.
3. Bake for 30 minutes, until the salmon flakes apart easily when pierced with a fork.

Serves 4

⊰[NUTS]⊱

Cooks have used almonds and other nuts creatively for centuries. The Romans pounded them into sauces for dressing meat, along with wine, honey, broth, herbs, and spices, which is pretty sophisticated stuff. But sometimes it's nice to just go back to the basics, and freshly roasted almonds with a simple seasoning of salt and pepper is ultimately just as satisfying as the most gourmet recipe.

SALT-AND-PEPPER ALMONDS ♩♩♩

1 tablespoon vegetable oil
1 teaspoon salt

1 teaspoon coarsely ground black
pepper
2 cups whole, raw almonds

1. Heat the oil in a large skillet. Add the salt, pepper, and almonds and toast over medium-high heat, stirring constantly, until the almonds are darkened and fragrant, about 5 minutes.

Makes 2 cups

MIXED FRESHLY ROASTED NUTS 🥄🥄🥄

1 cup almonds
1 cup walnuts
1 cup hazelnuts

1. Preheat the oven to 350°F. Spread the nuts on a baking sheet and roast for 12 minutes, stirring the nuts halfway through roasting, until fragrant and lightly browned. Cool the nuts on the baking sheet before transferring to an airtight container.

Makes 3 cups

GRAPES, PINEAPPLE, PEACHES, POMEGRANATES, MELONS

Use the fruits served at the Feast of the Three Sleepers to make a lovely fruit platter.

OVEN-ROASTED TOMATO MEDLEY 🥄🥄🥄

Spanish explorers introduced the tomato to Europe from South America, but like the potato, people hesitated to eat it, as it belongs to the deadly nightshade family. The British called the early yellow variety "golden apples" or "love apples."

2 cups halved golden cherry tomatoes
2 cups halved red cherry tomatoes
2 shallots, sliced
1 tablespoon olive oil
2 cloves garlic, minced
1 teaspoon dried basil
½ teaspoon salt
¼ teaspoon freshly ground black pepper

1. Preheat the oven to 450°F. Spread the golden and red tomatoes and shallots on a baking sheet.

2. Combine the olive oil, garlic, basil, salt, and pepper and pour over the vegetables. Mix well with your hands and spread the mixture out again.

3. Cook for about 30 minutes until the tomatoes are shriveled and a bit charred in spots.

Serves 4

THE FEAST OF THE DWARVES

· Pies · Sliced Calf's Tongue with Citrus Sage Sauce · Pigeons · Trifles ·

· Fruit Juice Ices · Raspberry Sorbet ·

Lucy wants to help the dwarves, but they are locked in the prison of their minds, Aslan tells her, "so afraid of being taken in that they cannot be taken out." That's why she can't help them see that they are in the beautiful outdoors; they're determined to believe they are in a dark, dirty, smelly stable. And they can't even enjoy the feast Aslan conjures for them: they are convinced not only that it's stable food, but also that the next dwarf got something better to eat, which sets them fighting with each other (*The Last Battle*, chapter 13).

⋯⊰⟦ PIES ⟧⊱⋯

A Sumerian tablet from before 2000 BC is inscribed with a recipe for chicken pie, so we know that pies have been around a long time. The Greeks and then the Romans cooked meat fillings enclosed in a flour-water paste, which sealed in juices and made the dish portable for traveling. In the Middle Ages, the crust was actually used as a container and was very tough, not really edible. A pie crust was called a coffin, or *coffyn*. A typical instruction in *The Forme of Cury* is: "Do it in a coffin and do it forth to bake well." Placing a lid just on top of the pie, as in the following recipes, is a more modern version.

BEEF PIE

1½ pounds extra-lean ground beef

3 tablespoons vegetable oil

1 onion, chopped

2 celery ribs, chopped

2 medium carrots, chopped

8 to 10 ounces mushrooms, sliced

2 garlic cloves, minced

2 tablespoons all-purpose flour

1½ cups chicken broth

2 tablespoons tomato paste

Salt, to taste

Freshly ground black pepper, to taste

1 sheet puff pastry

1 egg, beaten with 1 tablespoon
    water

1. Place a baking sheet in the oven and preheat the oven to 425°F. Brown the
    ground beef over high heat in a large skillet, using a wooden spoon to break up
    lumps. Transfer to a large plate.

2. Add the oil, onion, celery, carrots, and mushrooms to the skillet and cook over
    medium-high heat until the water evaporates. Continue cooking and stirring
    until well browned, about 15 minutes total cooking time.

3. Add the garlic and cook just until fragrant, a few seconds. Sprinkle the flour
    over the mixture and stir until combined. Stir in the chicken broth and tomato
    paste. Cook, stirring, until the mixture is thickened and bubbling, about 10
    minutes. Add the ground beef and stir to combine. Taste and adjust the sea-
    sonings with the salt and pepper.

4. Pour the mixture into a 2-quart baking dish. Drape the sheet of puff pastry
    over the filling. Tuck the ends under, brush the egg mixture over the top with a
    pastry brush, and cut slits for vents. Place the pie on the baking sheet and bake
    for 25 minutes, until golden brown.

Serves 8

Chicken Pot Pie

3 tablespoons vegetable oil

10 ounces mushrooms, sliced

1 onion, chopped

3 tablespoons all-purpose flour

2 cups chicken broth

Salt, to taste

Freshly ground black pepper, to taste

4 cups cooked cubed chicken (from
    about 1½ pounds raw boneless,
    skinless chicken breast)

12 ounces (about 3 cups) frozen
    mixed peas and carrots

1 sheet puff pastry

1. Adjust the oven rack to the middle position and preheat the oven to 425°F.
    While the oven is preheating, heat the oil in a large skillet. Add the mushrooms
    and onion and cook over high heat, stirring constantly, until well browned,
    about 10 minutes.

2. Sprinkle the flour over the mushroom-onion mixture and stir until well combined. Add the chicken broth and cook and stir until smooth and thick, about 10 minutes. Cook 5 to 7 minutes more to remove the raw starch flavor. Season with salt and pepper.

3. Stir in the chicken, peas, and carrots. Scrape the mixture into a 2-quart baking dish (such as a deep 8-inch square pan). Cover the filling with the puff pastry, tucking the edges under. Cut slits for vents. Bake for 30 minutes, until golden brown and bubbling. Allow to rest for 15 minutes before serving.

Serves 8

·∙≫[SLICED CALF'S TONGUE WITH CITRUS SAGE SAUCE 🥄🥄🥄]≪∙·

THANKS TO CHEF CHRIS KOCH FOR THIS RECIPE.

Tongue has always been a prized delicacy. The Talmud, a collection from the sixth century of rabbinic discussions about Jewish scripture and Jewish law, customs, and philosophy, mentions tongue in reference to Abraham, who served it to his wayfaring guests. *Mrs. Beeton's Book of Household Management* offers a way to distinguish a horse's tongue from an ox tongue, as some crooked people in the Victorian era out to make a quick buck tried to sell to unsuspecting buyers the cheaper horse's tongue. ("The horse's tongue may be readily distinguishable by a spoon-like expansion at its end," the author wrote.)

CALF'S TONGUE
3 tablespoons cider vinegar
2 tablespoons lemon juice
2 quarts water
1 tablespoon kosher salt
1 calf's tongue, about 1½ pounds

CITRUS SAUCE
¾ cup orange juice
½ cup honey
1 teaspoon dried sage
1 tablespoon lemon juice
½ teaspoon dried thyme
½ teaspoon dry mustard

1. Combine the vinegar, lemon juice, water, and salt in a pot. Add the tongue and bring to a boil. Reduce to a simmer and cook, covered, for about 1 hour or until tender. Remove the pot from the heat and let the tongue cool in the liquid.

2. Remove the skin from the tongue and the root end. Beginning at the tip, slice the tongue into ¼-inch-thick diagonal slices. Arrange the slices on a platter.

3. Combine the sauce ingredients in a small saucepan and bring to a boil. Reduce to a simmer for 5 minutes. Drizzle over the sliced tongue, reserving some for passing around at the table.

Serves 8

PIGEONS

Use the Pigeon Stew with Wood Sorrel recipe from the "Poggin the Dwarf Makes Breakfast" menu on page 30, and the Pigeon and Morel Pie recipe from the "Prince Rilian Orders Food for the Updwellers" menu on page 167.

TRIFLES

Early trifles started out as little more than boiled and flavored cream. By the 1700s, wine-soaked biscuits were placed in the bottom of the dish, custard was poured over them, and the whole thing was topped off with syllabub (a frothy confection made by whisking cream with wine or brandy or both). By the late nineteenth century, ordinary whipped cream was used as a topping, and the trifle as we know it was established.

CLASSIC ENGLISH TRIFLE

24 store-bought or homemade ratafia biscuits (recipe follows) or almond macaroons

2 tablespoons dry white sherry, optional
¼ cup raspberry jam, melted

1 recipe Custard (recipe follows,
    or use 1 packet instant vanilla
    pudding mix and follow the
    directions on the packet)
1 recipe Whipped Cream (recipe
    follows)

¼ cup toasted slivered almonds, for
    decorating
¼ cup golden raisins, for decorating
¼ cup candied mixed peel, for
    decorating

1. Break the biscuits into pieces and place in a 9- or 10-inch dish (glass is prettiest). Sprinkle the sherry, if using, over the biscuits and add the jam. Mix with a spoon directly in the pan and then smooth into a layer.

> To save time, you can buy the biscuits and use instant vanilla pudding instead of the custard.

2. Stir the custard to loosen it and spread it over the layer of biscuit mixture. Spread the whipped cream on top and sprinkle with the nuts, raisins, and candied peel. You can serve immediately or store in the refrigerator until ready to use. The trifle is best eaten the day it is made, but it can be eaten within 2 or 3 days. If you don't mind soggy biscuits, it will still be good within 1 week of making it.

Serves 8 to 10

RATAFIA BISCUITS

2 cups finely ground almonds
    (the almonds don't need to be
    blanched)
1 cup confectioners' sugar, sifted
2 egg whites, at room temperature

1 teaspoon pure almond extract
1 teaspoon pure vanilla extract
½ teaspoon salt
¼ teaspoon cream of tartar
¼ cup granulated sugar

1. Line 2 baking sheets with parchment paper and preheat the oven to 350°F.
2. Whisk the almonds and confectioners' sugar in a large mixing bowl and set aside. Using an electric beater fitted with the whisk attachment, beat the egg whites with the almond extract, vanilla extract, salt, cream of tartar, and granulated sugar until stiff peaks form.
3. Fold the egg white mixture into the almond mixture until a stiff batter forms. Using a small cookie scoop or teaspoon, portion out the dough 1 inch apart on the baking sheets. Bake for 12 minutes, rotating and switching the pans halfway through baking. The biscuits will spread and be pale. They will be very soft

when they come out of the oven, but they will set up as they cool (they will still be chewy). Transfer to wire racks to cool.

Makes about 30 biscuits

CUSTARD

2 cups milk	*3 tablespoons cornstarch*
⅓ cup sugar	*1½ teaspoons pure vanilla extract*
4 large egg yolks	

1. Heat the milk and sugar in a medium saucepan over medium heat, stirring until the sugar is dissolved. Continue cooking until steaming hot but not bubbling.

2. Whisk together the yolks and cornstarch until smooth. Pour in 1 cup of the hot milk mixture while constantly whisking, then pour the yolk mixture into the saucepan, stirring constantly. Cook, stirring constantly, until the mixture is thick and bubbling, about 5 minutes.

3. Remove from the heat and stir in the vanilla extract. Pour through a sieve to ensure a perfectly smooth custard.

WHIPPED CREAM

1 cup heavy cream	*1 teaspoon pure vanilla extract*
¼ cup confectioners' sugar	

1. Whip all the ingredients together until stiff peaks form.

APPLE TRIFLE 🥄🥄🥄

Isabella Beeton's recipe calls for a layer of applesauce, a layer of custard, and a layer of whipped cream. This version, with its sponge cake base, is more substantial, and, frankly, yummier.

1 recipe Sugar-Dusted Sponge Tea Cake (page 45) or store-bought pound or angel food cake	*1 recipe Custard (recipe follows) or 2½ cups store-bought instant vanilla pudding*
½ cup apple jelly, melted	*1 recipe Whipped Cream (recipe follows)*
1 recipe Apple Filling (recipe follows)	

1. Slice the cake into 1-inch pieces. Line the bottom of a serving dish (glass preferred) about 10 inches by 2 inches with the cake slices (a 9-inch springform pan also works, but doesn't look as pretty). Spread the melted jelly over the cake. Spread the apple filling over the jelly and then pour the custard over the filling.

2. Dollop the whipped cream over the top of the custard, or use a pastry bag to pipe mounds of cream over the custard. You can serve immediately or keep refrigerated until ready to use. This trifle is best eaten the day it is assembled, but it can be refrigerated up to 2 days after assembly, though the cake will get slightly soggy. If you don't mind soggy trifle, the dessert will keep for up to 1 week.

Serves 10

Apple Filling

2 sweet apples, such as Gala, peeled,
  cored, and chopped

Juice and zest of 1 lemon

2 tart apples, such as Granny Smith,
  peeled, cored, and chopped

⅓ cup brown sugar

1. Place all the ingredients in a medium or large saucepan and simmer, covered, until the apples are soft, about 30 minutes. Remove the lid, raise the heat to high, and cook until the water has boiled out, about 5 minutes, stirring to prevent scorching.

Custard

2 cups milk

⅓ cup sugar

4 large egg yolks

1 tablespoon cornstarch

1½ teaspoons pure vanilla extract

1. Heat the milk and sugar in a saucepan over medium heat, stirring until the sugar is dissolved. Continue cooking until steaming hot but not bubbling, about 5 minutes.

Variation for Adults:
Replace the vanilla in the custard with 2 tablespoons apple brandy.

2. Whisk together the yolks and cornstarch until smooth. Pour 1 cup of the hot milk mixture into the yolk mixture while constantly whisking, then pour the yolk mixture into the saucepan, stirring constantly. Cook, stirring constantly, until the mixture is thick and bubbling, about 5 minutes.

3. Remove from the heat and stir in the vanilla extract. Pour through a sieve to ensure a perfectly smooth custard.

WHIPPED CREAM

1 cup heavy cream
¼ cup sugar

1 teaspoon pure vanilla extract

1. Whip all the ingredients in a large mixing bowl until stiff peaks form.

·∘] FRUIT JUICE ICES ♪♪♪ [∘·

I've already written about the popularity of serving ices toward the middle and the end of elaborate meals. A typical Victorian dinner menu would include "dessert and ices" as the final course.

1 cup apple juice
½ cup pineapple juice
½ cup white grape juice
½ teaspoon orange extract, optional

3 to 4 drops red food coloring, or
more to reach desired shade,
optional

1. In a 2-cup measuring cup, mix all the ingredients together, including the orange extract and red food coloring, if using.
2. Pour the mixture into an ice cube tray and freeze until solid, about 6 hours or overnight. Crush 3 to 4 frozen cubes per serving in a blender. Serve immediately.

Serves 3 to 4

·∘] RASPBERRY SORBET ♪♪♪ [∘·

Did you know that the raspberry belongs to the rose family? The Greeks called the raspberry bush *idaeus* because lots of it grew on Mount Ida. There are two mountains of that name, one in Greece and one in Turkey, and both produce an abundance of raspberries. You will need an ice cream maker for this recipe.

24 ounces raspberries, fresh or   1¼ cups sugar
    frozen, thawed if frozen   1 cup water

1. Place the raspberries, sugar, and water in the bowl of a food processor. Process until smooth, 1 or 2 minutes.

2. Push the mixture through a sieve with a rubber spatula, stirring and pressing to extract as much juice as possible. Discard the pulp. Chill until cold.

3. Freeze in an ice cream maker according to the manufacturer's instructions. Transfer to an airtight container and freeze until firm.

4. Allow the sorbet to soften at room temperature for 15 minutes before serving

Makes about 4 cups

SOURCES

While I used the following sources for my research, any errors in historical fact are my own.

BOOKS

Apicius. *Cookery and Dining in Imperial Rome*. Translated by Joseph Dommers Vehling. New York: Dover Publications, 1977. www.gutenberg.org.

Beeton, Isabella. *Mrs. Beeton's Book of Household Management*. Oxford: Benediction Classics, 2010.

Boswell, James. *The Journal of a Tour to the Hebrides with Samuel Johnson*. London: Henry Baldwin for Charles Dilly. 1785.

Davidson, Alan. *The Oxford Companion to Food*. Oxford, New York: Oxford University Press, 2006.

Greweling, Peter P. *Chocolates and Confections at Home with the Culinary Institute of America*. Hoboken, NJ: John Wiley & Sons, 2010.

———. *Chocolates and Confections: Formula, Theory, and Technique for the Artisan Confectioner*. Hoboken, NJ: John Wiley & Sons, 2007.

Lewis, C. S. *The Chronicles of Narnia*. New York: HarperCollins Publishers, 2001.

Norwak, Mary. *English Puddings: Sweet and Savoury*. London: Grub Street, 2009.

Paston-Williams, Sara. *Good Old-Fashioned Puddings*. London: National Trust Books, 2007.

Pearson, Lu Emily. *Elizabethans at Home*. Stanford, California: Stanford University Press, 1957. www.books.google.com.

Pegge, Samuel. *The Forme of Cury*. London: J. Nichols, 1780. www.gutenberg.org.

Spencer, Colin. *British Food: An Extraordinary Thousand Years of History*. New York: Columbia University Press, 2002.

WEBSITES

library.thinkquest.org

www.bbc.co.uk/food/recipes

www.books.google.com

http.britainexpress.com/History/tea-in-britain.htm

www.britannia.com/cooking/recipes

www.cooksillustrated.com

www.foodtimeline.org

www.gutenberg.org

www.historicfood.com/Nesselrode%20Pudding%20Recipe.htm

www.wikipedia.com

INDEX

ABOUT THE AUTHOR

Dinah Bucholz is the author of the *New York Times* bestselling *Unofficial Harry Potter Cookbook*. Her second favorite thing in the world is creating recipes for the foods in her best-loved books and writing about them (her favorite thing is eating them). She lives in Philadelphia with her husband and four kids. She has never been to Narnia but plans to visit as soon as she finds the right wardrobe.

You can visit Dinah at www.dinabucholz.com to see photos of some of the foods featured in this book or just to say hello; she answers all her email.